HORROR, DEMONS AND PHILOSOPHY

RICK WOOD

BLOOD SPLATTER PRESS

Also By Rick Wood

The Sensitives
The Sensitives
My Exorcism Killed Me
Close to Death
Demon's Daughter
Questions for the Devil
Repent
The Resurgence
Until the End

Blood Splatter Books
Psycho B*tches
Shutter House
This Book is Full of Bodies
This Book is Full of More Bodies
Home Invasion
Haunted House
Woman Scorned
Sex Blood
He Eats Children

Cia Rose

When the World Has Ended
When the End Has Begun
When the Living Have Lost
When the Dead Have Decayed

The Edward King Series

I Have the Sight
Descendant of Hell
An Exorcist Possessed
Blood of Hope
The World Ends Tonight

Anthologies

Twelve Days of Christmas Horror
Twelve Days of Christmas Horror Volume 2
Roses Are Red So Is Your Blood

Standalones

When Liberty Dies
The Death Club

Sean Mallon

The Art of Murder
Redemption of the Hopeless

Chronicles of the Infected

Zombie Attack
Zombie Defence
Zombie World

Non-Fiction

How to Write an Awesome Novel

INTRODUCTION

Oh boy, do I love horror.

Just as much as I find demons fascinating.

And just as much as I love reading philosophy that both explores and challenges my atheistic belief systems.

And these are the three themes I plan to explore in this book.

Horror is a wonderful, bizarre, uncanny, absurd genre that shows us both the worst and best of humanity. Every genre, whether intentionally or unintentionally, explores and reflects the society and culture in which it is written—but horror does it unlike any other.

Why?

Because horror does not have the constraints of other genres.

If you read horror, then you can expect to have the most grotesque, nasty, extreme scenarios films or literature will allow. You can witness the unrealistic and realistic extremes of the depths of humans and monsters. And, each time this is done, a statement is being made about society—often intentionally, like in *Us* or *It Follows*, but sometimes unintentionally.

There are a vast array of subgenres, each able to provide you with the titillation you desire.

And, as is evidenced by the demonic horror series that launched my author career (*The Sensitives*), demons are one of my favourite themes to explore.

I love reading about the mythology and origins of demons. Without needing a belief in their existence, I can still attain great pleasure in learning which religion, from however many thousands of years ago, believed in which demon and for what purpose.

When you explore the origins of demons, you discover just how different those demons are to the way they are represen-tated in films or books. For example, Pazuzu from *The Exorcist* is, in the reality of demonic existence, very different from the vile, sexually aggressive demon depicted in the book and film. (If you wish to know how Pazuzu is different, you will have to read on...)

And I also love exploring philosophy, and the suggestions different theorists make about our world, whether I agree or disagree with them. For example, whilst Hobbs believes humans are good and society brings out our worst, Machiavelli believes humans are bad and society keeps us constrained; both of which are fascinating and contrasting points of view.

I debated long and hard about whether to include my athe-istic views in my discussion of philosophy, but I would find it hard not to. I know that many of my readers believe in the supernatural that I write about, but I do not, and contra-dicting the beliefs of the devout will often elicit a hugely nega-tive response. I am hugely critical of religion, and I found it difficult for this attitude not to come through in this book.

If you are an atheist also, you will undoubtedly agree with much that I say. If you are agnostic, you may enjoy the ideas I put forward as something to think about. If you are a theist, however, you may not like my opinions—if this is the case, I ask you to keep an open mind and accept my point of view. If you feel that you can't do this, then this may not be the book for you.

And so begins our exploration of horror, demons, and philosophy. And why not begin with the question that provokes such debate or bemusement when asked—why on earth do we like horror?

Horror 101: The Theories Behind Why We Love Horror

It makes sense, before I dive into any discussion of horror, that we pose the most simple and complex question of all: why do we love horror?

Explore this question on an internet message board and you will find many varied responses, from "because I just do" to "because I'm a sick fuck." Maybe some people will answer "because I liked The Exorcist when I was a kid", and maybe some will say "my dad introduced me to it." But none of these answers are actually answering the question.

Why did you like The Exorcist as a kid? Why did you like it when your dad introduced you to it? Why do you think it has anything to do with you being a 'sick fuck' when the horror audience features such a vast range of people from all walks of life, most of whom are not considered 'sick'?

Horror Studies is a field that is only just developing, mainly because of horror being a subject academics generally scoff at; it is a genre that only a few people have given deeper thought to. More recently, however, scholars are beginning to add to an educated discourse about horror, with real theories and discussion about what turns a film or book into horror, and why we enjoy it when it is theoretically so disturbing.

What makes horror into horror is an enormous question—one that would take a book much bigger than this to answer—but I can sum up most of my reading in a few sentences. Those sentences will not give justice to the depth of reading on the subject, but will still provide enough of an answer for us to proceed.

Horror is a genre that elicits the feeling of horror from an audience. It usually has a monster that is unnatural to the world it inhabits. It usually explores the boundaries that we take for granted, such as self/other and living/dead.

And now that is done, let's get to the question of *why* we love horror. There are three dominant theories that I am aware of, and I will start with the one I consider to be the weakest.

The first theory is that horror is for adolescent self-exploration. It teaches teenagers about appropriate sexual behaviour and societal taboos.

The obvious flaw: teenagers aren't the only fans of horror. And what of those who don't like horror—do they not learn about such concepts too?

Yes, teenagers will use horror to explore their emerging identity, just as they use music, clothing, and many other things to achieve this. It is not a sufficient explanation for me.

The second theory, and one that I would consider much stronger, uses the analogy of a rollercoaster. If we were to ask why someone might enjoy going on a rollercoaster, they might answer that it is to experience the thrills of adrenaline and danger whilst also knowing they are safe—which is precisely why one might enjoy horror. They can experience the worst atrocities known to humankind, and witness the deepest fears of their imaginations, all the while knowing they will not be hurt.

In his book, *Why Horror Seduces*, Mathias Clasen suggests

that it is part of our evolutionary psychology to practise dangerous scenarios; that our ancestors who practised such scenarios survived more often than those who didn't practise such scenarios, therefore making this a trait we have evolved to have.

In addition to this, Noel Carroll, in his book *Horror and Philosophy*, goes as far as to say that an audience's reaction to horror is make believe; that the audience is playing along, if you will. This may be true of some audiences, but I have also witnessed experiences of genuine fear. For example, those people who vomited after seeing *The Exorcist* for the first time —as bizarre as that reaction was, they probably weren't 'make believing' their puke. Even so, Carroll is onto something—if we pretend these fears are real so we can explore them safely, perhaps we also pretend our fear itself is real, thus allowing us to safely explore what we would not wish to realistically confront.

Horror is one of the genres best known to reflect society. For example, in 50s and 60s American horror movies, the monster was usually an alien threat, reflecting America's fear of being attacked by foreign invaders. In the 80s and 90s, the monster was usually hidden within suburban America, showing how the fear had changed from an outside threat to an inside threat, exploring what depravity may be hidden behind the perfect image of the model American. Horror allows society to confront what it fears.

It is perhaps too soon to make broad conclusions about what today's movies say about what society fears, but we can make a few suggestions: *Get Out* refers to the alienation felt by the black community, *Unfriended* refers to the fear of being absorbed in technology and social media, whilst *Mother* shows the destruction we are causing the earth and the environment.

I believe this is a strong explanation—but it is the third and final theory that I buy into the most.

In the early 1900s, psychoanalyst Sigmund Freud made some suggestions for what dreams are: that they show what we repress in everyday life. Whilst I am dubious about this explanation of dreams, and whilst many of his theories are discounted by modern day critics, I find his theory that we must repress much of our animal nature hard to argue with.

We are born with animal instinct, just like any other animal; but unlike other animals, we are expected to quell many of our instincts to fit in with society. For example, evidence shows we are not naturally monogamous animals, so to be faithful to our spouse, we must repress sexual cravings. Evidence also suggests that most of us are capable of murder, and that most of us have harboured at least one murder fantasy (see *The Murderer Next Door* by David Buss), but most of us do not go onto kill. We must control such impulses through the act of repression.

Robin Wood, probably one of the most notable horror theorists, suggested in his 1980s essay *An Introduction to the American Horror Film* that horror allows us to explore what we repress in a safe environment.

When you watch an audience watching a slasher, they are rooting for the protagonist. But, when the killer disposes of some less important protagonists, they are also clearly cheering for that antagonist.

Why?

Because we explore what we repress to obey social norms and avoid deviant behaviour, and in witnessing a character perform the actions we repress, we vicariously explore them. Many censors claim that horror makes us violent, but I would suggest that the opposite is true. Yes, there will be the few people who might commit violence and claim to have been encouraged by violence in horror, but most horror lovers are healthy human beings who hold down jobs and love their families. Perhaps, by unleashing what we repress through horror, we can function better in everyday life. We have explored that side of us through horror, and so do not need to explore it in real life. In this sense, horror makes us better citizens.

Within this theory is the concept of catharsis—the release one has when they let go of powerful emotions. It is a satisfaction one gains from watching or reading horror, and letting out all that they hold inside.

If everyone were to watch horror, then perhaps the violence in the world would decrease. But if that happened, and there was nothing left to fear, what would horror auteurs use to make horror about?

And now, since we have established some of the key concepts behind our love of horror, we can move onto some of my own musings and ramblings, and explore what makes horror such a fascinating genre.

THE REAL MONSTER

The monster is usually what sets horror apart from other genres.

Not just that there is a monster—but the status of the monster, and the reaction of the characters. For example, there are monsters in the Disney movie *Monsters Inc*, but it's not horror. Why? Because the monsters are meant to be a part of that fictional world. In horror, whether it is a zombie, ghost, demon, vampire, or killer, the monster's presence and their intentions are seen as unnatural to the world it inhabits. In addition, the characters are usually horrified by the presence of the monster's threat.

But this is a general view of the monster. We can gain bigger insight from the monster in the form of a question— one that tells us a lot about society. The question is as so:

Who is the real monster?

Yes, the monster is presented as horrible and threatening— but, as I have found in most horror, it's not as simple as that.

Let's go back a few centuries and look at some of the first

major works in horror, starting with *Frankenstein*. Dr Franken-stein makes a monster out of dead body parts. That monster is a threat to the world it should not inhabit. But, when we examine the situation more closely, I wonder whether that monster is really the monster.

Frankenstein's monster was created against his will. He is struggling to come to terms with his existence. He is desper-ately lonely and in need of a mate. This isn't the will of a monster—this is the will of a human.

But what of Dr Frankenstein? He created something unnatural to this world. He did it for personal gain. He did it without considering the repercussions. Are his actions not monstrous?

And what of the town folk? The ones who see what Dr Frankenstein has created and view it as an ugly, horrible crea-ture, prompting them to turn on it. They are judging this crea-ture's appearance and turning violent as a result. Are their actions not monstrous?

As we see, the 'monster' Dr Frankenstein has created might not be the actual monster, but Dr Frankenstein and the town folk most likely are.

Another book of a similar time period is *Dr Jekyll and Mr Hyde*. Dr Jekyll takes a potion, and it turns him into a hideous, violent creature. We assume Mr Hyde is the monster, yes?

But what created Mr Hyde? We could say it was the potion, but is it that simple?

The book was written in a Victorian society that was noto-riously repressed. This society maintained the notion of the Victorian gentleman, and how such a man should behave. He was meant to be gentle, noble, silent, stern, emotionless, and, most of all, restrained. When one lives in a society where they are expected to have no emotions, what happens to those emotions?

Dr Hyde was created by the unrealistic expectations of the

class and society Mr Jekyll was in—so who was the real monster? Dr Hyde, an inevitable product of a society that placed unrealistic expectations upon him, or the society who created the monster through forcing Mr Jekyll to repress his emotions?

Let's have a look at a few more recent examples.

In *28 Days Later*, we witness a post-apocalyptic society where the zombies—people injected with the rage virus—try to kill anyone they find. Those zombies are evidently the monsters, yes?

But what happens when the male and two females that survive find an army base and believe they have finally found protection? The soldiers force the man to step aside so they can rape the two women, thus satisfying the sexual frustration they have felt being in an army base with no women.

So who's the real monster here? The one who's injected with a rage virus and can't help their actions—or the potential rapists?

In Paul Tremblay's fantastic novel, *A Head Full of Ghosts*, we witness a family who agree to be on a reality television show that features their (supposedly) possessed daughter being exorcised. We are never sure whether she is really possessed, which leads to us questioning whether the girl is the monster, or the demon inside of her is the monster. Further to this, her parents agree to have her situation, whether it is a mental breakdown or demonic possession, broadcast on television to solve their financial problems. Maybe it is them who are the monsters, as they exacerbate their daughter's condition for profit.

In Rob Zombie's remake of *Halloween*, we witness the origins of Michael Myers. A killer who is ruthless and determined to kill anyone in his way – surely, he must be the monster?

Alas, maybe not.

During the origins of Michael Myers' story, we see his stepfather being abusive toward him, his sister rejecting him, and his mother failing to protect him. Then he is helped by a doctor that uses his experience of treating Michael to profit from his book (as is explored further in Rob Zombie's sequel.) When he is grown up, Michael is bullied and tormented by one of the people working in the sanatorium where he lives. All of these people have created Michael Myers, the killer. All of these were monsters long before Michael Myers became the monster.

And, as a final example, let's look at *The Last Exorcism*. A pastor, who performs fraudulent exorcisms, is invited to help a girl who is, as we discover, possessed for real—all whilst being filmed by a documentary crew. His fraudulent exorcisms normally act as a placebo, helping the family and the 'possessed' to rid themselves of the fake demon through the belief that the demon is gone. The pastor receives money for this.

The demon inside of the girl is the obvious monster in this film, but if we delve a little deeper, we find examples of monstrous behaviour in others. The pastor, who takes advantage of people who are in a vulnerable situation. The father, who secludes his daughter on the farm and fills her head with toxic religious ideals. The documentary crew, who wish to film people being taken advantage of.

It appears that we are all capable of being the monster, but that it is easier to point our fingers at the "other."

Which leads me onto the next section of the book—demons. Demonic horror is my favourite genre, and has been both the focus of my studies, and the genre of many of the books that have allowed me to make a living as an author. But, as we are about to find out, whilst many demonic horror films use 'real' demons, the actual mythology of these demons is often different to that which is presented in the films.

The Truth Behind the Demons from the Movies

It was in February 2020 that I began my PhD in Literary and Critical Studies—and, as I write this book, I'm making good progress.

My aim has been to contribute new knowledge to horror studies. Demonic horror has always fascinated me and, as a result, I chose to research how demonic horror reflects the society in which it is written.

Of course, I did not know just how much I was going to learn about the topic.

I've analysed, in the most minute detail, many demonic horror novels. I have read various theories about the value of demonic horror and how demons are presented. And I have discovered just how much demons allow us to learn about the world.

In modern day, demons are used in books and movies as Freudian entities that show us what we repress. The demons act in a way that displays the ugly side of the world that we deny.

Throughout history, however, demons have been religion's way of controlling the population. Police weren't brought in to enforce the law in the UK or US until the 1800s—so how were the authorities meant to control the inhabitants of society back then?

By using demons to warn people off unwanted behaviour through fear of what those demons might do.

If they came up with a demon for promiscuity, a demon for lewdness, and a demon for slovenliness—then those that fear these demons will do all they can to avoid them, i.e., being less promiscuous, lewd or slovenly (this is discussed in more detail in a later chapter).

I find these demons fascinating. I love their mythology, their stories, and the way they are presented. In fiction, they are incredibly entertaining antagonists that make for fantastic books and movies. In non-fiction, they are historical artefacts to be studied, teaching us about the people who created the background to these demons.

It may also not surprise you that, in doing my research, I was taken aback by how many movies have portrayed the demons they deploy incorrectly.

In fact, most of the demons utilised in horror show very little research on the filmmaker's part. There are so many layers to these entities that are portrayed as pure evil. Quite a few of these evil beings, in fact, can be seen quite differently dependent upon context, or which source you use for your information.

The notion of definite good and definite evil was invented by more recent religious interpretations. Greek gods, Egyptian gods, and gods of forgotten religions, such as religions of the Akkadians and Babylonians, were not categorically good or bad. This was also the case with many of the demons; there are interpretations of these demons that add layers to their existence.

Before I explain these layers and the mythology of these

demons, I think it is appropriate to highlight my primary sources.

There have been various grimoires written on demons throughout the last few thousand years. Grimoires are books on magic, whether it be spells or a textbook—and, in this case, I have looked closely at a set of anonymously written grimoires called Lemegeton Clavicula Salomonis—otherwise known as The Lesser Key of Solomon. It is a text from either the 1500s or the 1600s, depending on which source you believe, and is divided into five books:

- Ars Goetia
- Ars Theurgia-Goetia
- Ars Pauilina
- Ars Almedal
- Ars Notoria

Most of the demons I have discussed in this book feature in Ars Goetia, so that is the book I have used the most. It was named Goetia as it derives from the ancient Greek word meaning witchcraft. It is a medieval text on demonology that provides the background to the 72 spirits of Solomon and how to summon them.

(Solomon was a king from the Old Testament who was fascinated by demons, and there are many reports on how he used demons for his own benefit, such as building temples. It is his legend that prompted his name to be used in the book's title. He was also considered to be a major prophet in the Quran.)

There have been two other major texts published on demonology that I will use. The first is Pseudomonarchia Daemonum—also known as The False Monarchy of Demons. This text was published in 1563 by a Dutch occultist called Johann Weyer.

The second is Dictionnaire Infernal, a text published in 1863 that provides a guide to various demons.

I have also used the Bible and other religious scriptures when appropriate, as well as various online sources that discuss the origins of demons.

I should also emphasise that I am not looking at these texts as having a factual basis, but as historical texts highlighting the belief in the mythology of demons throughout time. My approach to demonology is not about whether they are a real and present danger, but what they can tell us about the world in which they were created.

In the next few chapters, you are about to discover the essential information you need to start your journey into demonology. Next time someone discusses how demons are evil and how the demon Pazuzu in *The Exorcist* is scary, you can correct them—because, as it turns out, Pazuzu isn't that bad a guy.

I hope you find it as interesting to read as I found researching it.

Pazuzu From The Exorcist

Despite the demon in *The Exorcist* introducing itself as the devil at one point in the movie, it was never the intention of William Peter Blatty, the book's author, that Regan was possessed by The Devil. The Devil is the supreme ruler of Hell, after all, and just as Blatty once said, why would The Devil bother with a little girl?

It is in fact Pazuzu who Blatty intended to be the demon. Also called Fazuzu and Kazuz, the demon is reported to have the feet of an eagle, paws of a lion, head of a dog, tail of a scorpion, bulging eyes, and four wings. Many sources also portray him as having the erect penis of a serpent. He was the king of the demons of the wind, ruled the hot desert winds of Arabia, and was the son of the god Hambi—who, in Sumerian and Akkadian mythology, was the god of evil.

But, despite his terrifying appearance and backstory, Pazuzu might not be as bad a guy as Linda Blair portrayed him.

Pazuzu is unlike most of the demons in this book as he predates Christianity, and comes from Assyrian and Babylonian mythology—with the old, middle and neo-Assyrian empires dating from 2024 BC to 609 BC, also known as Akkadia.

The beginning of *The Exorcist* foreshadows what is to come when the exorcist appears at an archaeological dig in Northern Iraq, and he comes across a statue of Pazuzu, which he sees as an omen. This is an accurate place for him to find such a statue, as Assyria and Babylonia would roughly be modern-day Iraq, as well as parts of Iran, Kuwait, Syria and Turkey.

What is not accurate, however, is the ominous feeling of the statue. The statue of Pazuzu was actually something many people had in their homes—you can even find a 15cm statue of Pazuzu in the Louvre. And there is, in fact, a good reason to have a statue of Pazuzu in your home, especially if you are pregnant or have a young child.

During the eighth to sixth centuries BC, Pazuzu was known to have been in constant battle with a demon called Lamashtu—a demon who, funnily enough, I researched and used in my novel *I Have the Sight*.

Lamashtu is a demoness, and an ugly one at that—with a lion's head, donkey's teeth, a hairy body, bloody hands, and long fingernails. She brings harm to pregnant women and newborn babies, often killing unborn children by tapping on the mother's belly or stealing infants from their cots.

It was said that, because of their constant conflict, Pazuzu would scare Lamashtu away and send her back to Hell. This was why many pregnant women kept statues of Pazuzu in their homes, and often wore Pazuzu as an amulet or pendant. They believed this demon would protect their young. Which is in huge contrast to the demon's portrayal in *The Exorcist*—where the demon plagues young Regan.

Then again, the word 'demon' only has evil connotations in more recent millennia—the Greek word daimon actually meant 'spirit.' The nature of whether the demon is good or evil depends entirely on their context, as you will find out with several demons in this book.

Despite this, the name Pazuzu has had some negative connotations in recent times. A man called Pazuzu Ilah Algared, a self-proclaimed Satanist, was charged with first-degree murder in October 2014 after remains of two drifters, who'd disappeared in 2009, were found buried in his backyard. This Pazuzu never stood trial, as he committed suicide a year after he was charged.

The Exorcist also didn't include that Pazuzu was a demon known for bringing famine and locusts, rather than tormenting girls on the brink of puberty and making them sexually aggressive toward their mothers. It makes me wonder why Blatty used such a demon when there are so many demons associated with tormenting children.

Maybe even Lamashtu herself, for example.

Abalam From The Last Exorcism

Also known as Abali, Abalam is from Christian mythology—although he also appears in the Quran, but not as a demon. Islam once regarded him as an angel, and now regards him as a jinn—which are hard creatures to explain. Some mythology describes a jinn as a genie, but this is slightly inaccurate. In Islamic mythology, a jinn can be associated with evil, such as with possession and illness, but can also be associated with good, through being supportive.

In Christian mythology, Abalam was either a king or a prince of Jinnestan, which is a large sector in Hell, also known as the country of the jinn. It is divided into two sections—the Badait Coldare (desert of the monsters) and the Badiatealgim (desert of demons).

Abalam features in the Ars Goetia, not in its own section, but as part of Paimon's section—who was the demon used in *Hereditary*, and is covered in that chapter. Ultimately, Abalam is subservient to Paimon, and will appear as one of two aides when Paimon is summoned. Some sources interpret Paimon and Abalam as the same demon, though most do not believe this to be true.

The use of Abalam in *The Last Exorcism* is interesting, as they have not chosen a high-ranking demon. One would think that, considering the character Nell gives birth to this demon in a fiery, messianic scene, they would choose a high-ranking demon that would bring forth much destruction into the world.

Not that Abalam isn't a bad guy who will bring torment to the world, but he's a lackey. A prince, not a king. Someone else's bitch.

Surely, he would possess Nell to pave the way for Paimon to come next? Perhaps that would have been a better plot for *The Last Exorcism Part Two*, the sequel to the brilliant original, which we shall pretend never happened.

The Six Demons in The Exorcism of Emily Rose

This film, which features a priest on trial for neglect of a young woman, pleads that he is innocent as he was trying to save her with an exorcism—an exorcism which, through the eyes of the law, was a harmful act.

This film is based on the true case of Annelise Michael. In the film, Emily Rose claims to be possessed by six demons, but in reality, Annelise claimed to be possessed by even more—the most noticeable entity that was omitted from the movie being Hitler.

Still, I am focussing on the film, and the six demons that were named in one of the film's most intense exorcism scenes, and I will go through the background to each of them here.

First Demon: The Demon That Possessed Cain

Cain is a figure from the Bible, featured in the Book of Genesis, and is commonly known as the first ever murderer, and he who committed the first act of evil.

Cain was the firstborn son of Adam and Eve, born after

they were supposedly exiled from the Garden of Eden, and had a brother named Abel. Both brothers were farmers, and routinely offered their crops to God—Cain offering his vegetation, and Abel offering meat. Cain became intensely jealous when God seemed to prefer Abel's offering and, as a result, killed Abel. When God asks Cain where Abel is, most likely already knowing the answer, Cain replies, "I don't know. Am I my brother's keeper?"

God did not kill Cain, and instead provided him with a far worse fate. God told Cain that his crops would no longer grow, meaning that he no longer had purpose, and that he must become "a restless wanderer of the earth." No one was allowed to kill Cain as this would end his suffering, and God made sure of this by saying that "anyone who kills Cain will suffer vengeance seven times over"—so if they avenged Cain once, they would be avenged seven times. Adam and Eve had another son that took his place, whom they called Seth.

As Cain is the first person in biblical history to commit an evil act, many traditional Christians believe him to be the originator of evil, and that he is the person who introduced violence and greed into humanity.

God also marked him with 'The Mark of Cain' so he was easily identifiable. The Bible does not indicate what this mark looks like, but the TV series *Supernatural* featured their interpretation of the mark in series nine and ten. It had two dots, and what looked like a demented smile coloured in black. The show stated that it was a deadly curse to have marked on you.

As with any area of the Bible, there are various interpretations and several questions about the story. For example, the Bible never explains why God rejected Cain's offering for Abel's. However, the Midrash, a critical interpretation of the Bible by ancient Judaic authorities, offers the theory that Cain intentionally held back his best meat.

There are some, however, who question the categorisation of good and evil in this story.

For example, why is God demanding their best crops as sacrifices in the first place? What kind of god creates a world where his subservients must give up their best possessions to worship him? Surely that's showing the same arrogance many demons are accused of?

There are also many people who believe that The Mark of Cain is not unlucky. It protected Cain from being murdered and kept him safe for all his days. And yes, he was a restless wanderer—but so was Cain in Kung Fu, so was Clark Kent as he tried to figure out his place in the world, and so are many great characters in film and literature with troubled pasts.

After all, Cain never had to work at growing crops again, did he?

SECOND DEMON: THE DEMON THAT POSSESSED NERO

Nero was the fifth emperor of Rome, living from 37 to 68 AD. His real father died when he was two, and his mother remarried Claudius, the emperor, who subsequently adopted him, and Nero ended up succeeding his adoptive father at seventeen. This is another figure who has very different stories told about him, dependent upon your source.

Many say he was a ruler of the people, who favoured the lower classes and tried to get rid of the death penalty—whilst others say he was a tyrant who killed his mother and his wife, along with many Christians.

First, let's look at the positive side of Nero.

He was very much into cultural life and had many amphitheatres built. He encouraged athletic games, as well as the arts, and even dabbled in acting and poetry himself. He banned capital punishment, allowed slaves to make complaints against their owners, and pardoned several people who plotted against him.

He was also one of the very few rulers who annoyed the upper class by favouring the lower class. He preferred 'the people' over 'the elite.'

Christianity claims he persecuted and killed Christians; though one can understand why someone of this era disliked Christians when those Christians were killing their way into dominance. In fact, Christianity is only the dominant religion today because Christians have committed many bouts of genocide over the past 2,000 years. They slaughtered Pagans a few hundred years after Christ was (supposedly) born, just as they continued to slaughter any other religion that grew in popularity in the centuries that followed, such as the Cathars. (There is more on this in the later chapter 'Alternatives to Religion: Shakespeare and Philosophy.') Just imagine it—if Pagans hadn't lost their battle with the Catholics almost two millennia ago, you would be celebrating Pagan rituals instead of Christian ones. (Saying that, many Christian celebrations are stolen from Pagans anyway, such as Winter Solstice instead of Christmas, and Samhain instead of Halloween.)

Now let's look further at the negative implications of Nero. If we ignore the hypocrisy, we can delve into what Christianity claims about this man.

After the fire of 64 AD, known as The Great Fire of Rome, two-thirds of Rome was destroyed. Nero blamed this on the Christians and killed a bunch of them. This claim is made by Christian author Tertullian, who lived from 155 to 220 AD, and Lactantius, who lived from 250 to 325 AD.

Many people claim he set off the fire so he could rebuild Rome with his artistic image, and blaming Christians was a diversion tactic—though this theory has been widely disputed, as Nero was reported to have been located much further south at the time of the fire. Also, I'm not sure how Tertullian and Lactantius would know when they were born a century or so later.

Christians also claimed that Nero executed the apostles Peter and Paul, though there are several versions of this claim. Some say Peter was crucified upside down, some say Paul was beheaded, and some say Paul was shown mercy after God commanded Nero to knock off the whole killing Christians thing.

The most prophetic reports on Nero are by a prophetess called Sibylline Oracles. Fourteen of her books written in the sixth and seventh century AD survived, and in both books five and eight, she discusses the depths of Nero's destruction. She believed his acts toward Christians were so awful that he would return as the antichrist. In fact, some scholars believe that the number 666 in the Book of Revelations 17:1-18 is code for Nero.

I guess, as ever, it depends on who you choose to believe.

THIRD DEMON: THE DEMON THAT POSSESSED JUDAS ISCARIOT

Now, if you thought Nero's good and bad side were debatable, you just wait—it's time to learn about Judas!

The term Judas nowadays is used to describe someone who betrays their friends. Judas himself was Jesus's most infamous disciple; the Bible tells us how Judas betrayed Jesus to the Roman authorities, who subsequently crucified him. There is very little else we know about Judas aside from this supposed betrayal.

His name is also a giveaway—surnames back then don't work as they do now, and usually had 'the' between the forename and surname, making him Judas the Iscariot. The meaning of Iscariot has been debated, with one interpretation relating it to the Latin sicdarius, which meant murderer.

Judas is mentioned several times in religious literature, though with subtle differences in each story.

The Gospel of Mark claims to not know Judas's motive.

The Gospel of Matthew claims Judas did it for thirty pieces of silver, then returned the money and hung himself.

The Gospel of Luke and The Gospel of John both claimed Satan possessed Judas.

He has also featured in the fourteenth-century poem, Dante's Inferno, where he is in the depths of Hell with Caesar's assassins, Brutus and Cassius.

He is also in Islamic literature, in which he lies to the Jews to defend Jesus. In fact, an Arab geographer from the 1300s called Al-Dimashqi, claimed that Judas assumed Jesus's likeness and took his place.

There is, however, a newer interpretation of Judas's motive. Some believe that Judas carried out Jesus's instructions so Jesus could endure Hell for the sake of humanity. As controversial as this claim is, there has been a significant discovery made to back it.

For a long time, many Christians have denied that there were further gospels omitted from the Bible. Despite some of these being found, those who are devoutly religious continue to deny that they are genuine.

But it makes sense, doesn't it? That there would be several accounts of these events, and the church would have chosen the gospels that furthered their own narrative. In fact, there is a suggestion that they did not make the decision to portray Jesus as godly and omnipotent until centuries after his supposed birth.

Of course, you can just imagine the reaction of the devout

when The Gospel of Judas was discovered in a codex by an Egyptian antiquities dealer in 1978. In fact, the reception was so negative that the gospel remained untouched in a safety deposit box until 2000, when it was finally translated, before being released in 2006.

And for those that claim Judas's gospel is not genuine, St. Irenaeus of Lyon, who appeared to have knowledge of it, referred to in the second century. It seems that, 1,800 years later, covering your eyes, shaking your head, and shouting "not listening" is still the same preferred technique by some religious zealots.

In his gospel, Judas tells a different story. During Passover, Jesus takes Judas aside and reveals that he has secret knowledge about God, and says that Judas will understand better than the other apostles. Jesus tells Judas to report him to the Roman authorities so Jesus can escape his material body in which he is trapped.

The gospel also included a discourse between Judas and Jesus's brother, James, who had concerns about Judas being crucified, and asked for reassurance that Judas would still ascend to the highest heaven.

If this is true, then Judas was Jesus's most loyal devotee. He has martyred his name and agreed to be portrayed in infamy throughout history purely to obey his messiah's wishes. That is incredible loyalty.

But, in a world where even the non-disputed gospels can't actually agree on Judas's motives, I guess we're never going to have an answer.

FOURTH DEMON: LEGION

Legion is a term for a group of demons. Normally, when you read about a demon in the Ars Goetia, you're told how many legions of demons this prince of king commands—for example, Laiman commands 25 legions. Some other sources say that each legion contains 6,666 demons. Johann Weyer, an occultist that lived from 1515 to 1588, claimed that there were 72 princes/kings commanding legions—which would leave a total of 7,405,926 demons.

The reference in *The Exorcism of Emily Rose*, however, refers to a specific legion of demons in the Bible story where Jesus performs an exorcism; what is known as 'The Miracle of the Swine.'

The story is told in three gospels—Mark 5:1-13, Luke 8:26-33 and Matthew 8:28-32, but is not in The Gospel of John. Matthew does not name the demons, but both Mark and Luke refer to them as Legion—which is an important part of the Rites of Exorcism. Once the exorcist has the name of the demon, they have control over them, and it is therefore important that we witness Jesus learning the name of his opponent.

The story tells how of Jesus and his apostles entered a country called Gergesa—which was on the eastern side of the Sea of Galilee Palso, also called Lake Tiberas, which is in Israel. He saw a man writhing around and unable to be kept still by chains —as noted in Mark's gospel: "no one could bind him, not even with chains", "he tore chains apart and broke irons on his feet", "cry out and cut himself with stones."

Jesus asks for the demon's name and the demon says, "we are legion, for we are many", then they beg Jesus to put them into a group of pigs in a nearby field. Jesus obliges and transfers the demons into the pigs, who then run down the field and drown themselves in a baconesque mass suicide, as they believed that demons don't like water. Pigs are also seen as filthy animals in Judaism, and therefore are more deserving of being possessed by filthy demons.

This event has been interpreted by theologist Augustine of Hippo (354-430) and Italian friar Thomas Aquinas (1225-

1274) as meaning that Christians have no duty to animals. Of course, many modern-day Christians dispute this.

Either way, it makes me wonder what demon-bacon would taste like.

FIFTH DEMON: BELIAL

Belial's name derives from the Hebrew 'beli ye-al', meaning 'without worth'. The context of his name in the Bible, however, may have been misinterpreted. In the Geneva Bible—the translation of the bible that precedes the King James version we use today, the Bible referred to 'men of Belial.' The more recent translation doesn't refer to the demon Belial at all, and translates it as 'worthless men.'

Variations of his name are also used in the Old Testament when referring to those that are immoral and disobedient to God, such as Eli and Nabal. He is also referred to in the New Testament in 2 Corinthians 6:15, which has several translations. Using the New Matthew Bible's translation, Paul the Apostle asks, "What concord hath Christ with Belial? On what part has he who believes with an infidel?"

In this quote, Paul the Apostle questions how a follower of Christ could ever be in harmony with someone who doesn't believe in God—as it's much like having an allegiance with Belial. However, translations of the word Belial vary. Some sources interpret Paul the Apostle as using Belial meaning worthless, some interpret him as referring to the demon Belial, and some interpret Belial as a reference to The Devil.

The Ars Goetia is clearer on how it views Belial, describing him as deceptively beautiful and with a soft voice. Hebrew lore often believes him to have been the second angel created after Lucifer, but fell to Hell because of his evil and his lies. He appears as two beautiful angels on a chariot being pulled by dragons, creating wickedness and guilt—often through sexual perversion, fornication, and lust. Honestly, he sounds like my kind of guy.

The Dictionnaire Infernal says that Belial—spelt Beliall in this case—was created immediately after Lucifer, and helped to seduce many to the 'dark side.'

Belial is also featured in the Dead Sea Scrolls—a set of ancient Jewish scrolls found in the Qumran Caves, which are in the Judean desert, from 1946 onwards.

These scrolls state that Belial is the Leader of the Sons of Darkness. 'The Sons of Darkness" are those "who transgress the covenant"—meaning those who serve another God.

The scroll contains a prophecy that there will be a war between The Sons of Light and The Sons of Darkness, and that the darkness will be destroyed, and light will live for eternity.

Honestly, I think I'd prefer to worship Belial than a god who seems to condemn you as evil if you don't assert that he is your one and only God. But hey—what do I know? I'm just a Belial kind of guy...

SIXTH DEMON: LUCIFER

And, finally, the ruler of Hell himself. Though, as we all know, he wasn't always the king of the underworld.

The name Lucifer itself predates Christianity and is associated with Venus. Lucifer was the son of Roman Goddess Aurora, who was the Goddess of Dawn, and it wasn't until later that Christianity associated the name with The Devil.

Back in the day, before all this evil malarky started, Lucifer was one of God's earliest creations, known in some sources as Helel, and had the title Morning Star—the name Lucifer itself is Latin for 'light bringer.' He was the twin brother of Michael, and was one of God's most beautiful angels, with only God being superior.

Lucifer, however, couldn't just accept God's will. He wanted to know why God did things, and he grew increasingly annoyed at receiving cryptic answers to his questions. He disliked that God had a plan for people, and believed that people should be able to act of their own free will. He began to grow contempt toward humans as God devoted all his attention to developing them.

In the end, Lucifer grew to see God as a tyrannical ruler, so rebelled against him and tried to overthrow him. He lost, and God banished him to Hell, along with Lilith—Adam's second wife, who had joined Lucifer.

There is actually very little written about Lucifer in the Bible, and most sources that teach us about his story are from legend and literature, such as *Dante's Inferno* or John Milton's story *Paradise Lost*. The only Bible reference is in Isaiah 14:12, which reads "How have you fallen from heaven, morning star, son of the dawn! You have been cast down to the earth, you who once laid low the nations."

The Mormon interpretation of Lucifer differs slightly, and describes him as a son of Elohim and brother of Yahweh. Elohim is God and Yahweh is Jesus—so this implies that Lucifer was part of the family. He became obsessed with pride and tried to take over the family, but lost the disagreement and was exiled to Outer Darkness.

Of course, it wasn't until the second and third century that Lucifer was linked with the name Satan. In the Dictionnaire Infernal, Lucifer is not Satan, but is in fact a higher ranked demon, with Satan being his lieutenant. This text tells us that Lucifer was evoked on a Monday—perhaps this is why Mondays are always so horrible! He has many tricks, one of the most notable being that he removes the brooms that witches ride on to the sabbath—the little rascal—then gives those witches rides on his shoulders, as was attested by the Witches of Moira from Sweden in 1672. Contrary to the belief of him

being this hideous being, he appears with the figure of a beautiful child—when pissed off, however, he has a fiery face,
though this text says he is "nothing monstrous."

Either way, if I had to choose between having a beer with
God, or with Lucifer—I know who I'd rather have a bit of
banter with!

Baal from The Rite

Also known as Bael, Baell and Ba'al, his name means 'the lord', and whether Baal is a demon or a god will often depend on what you're reading.

If he is a demon, then he must be a powerful one, as he is the first demon to be mentioned in the Ars Goetia, which describes him as a king that rules in the east and makes one go invisible. He rules over 66 legions, and has a vague appearance —sometimes appearing as a cat, or a toad, or a man, or all three at once.

He is also mentioned in various sources, including:

- Dictionnaire Infernal, where he is referred to as "the head of the infernal powers."
- The Zohar, a piece of Jewish literature that acts as a commentary on the Torah, in which he has an equal rank to archangel Raphael.
- In the Bible, in Judges 2:10-15, where Baal is referred to in the plural sense, but this may be a mistranslation—in ancient Semiotic languages Baal meant 'lord' and 'owner', and we may not

fully understand how the word has changed over time.

- On various tablets uncovered in an ancient city on North Syria from 1929 onwards that date back to the second and third century.
- And in The Grimoire of Pope Honorius—which was written by Pope Honorius III, who lived 1150-1227.

Baal is often referred to as the agricultural and fertility god/demon of Canaan—Canaan being a region in the Ancient Near East that's mentioned a lot in the Bible, and is now roughly somewhere in the Middle East. Baal would engage in battle with Mot—a West Semitic god of the dead, also known simply as 'Death.' It was said that if he won, the land would have seven years of fertility, and if he lost, the land would have seven years of death and sterility.

As the legend went, Baal defeated Mot, but the crops withered and died anyway—that is, until his sister Anoth, The Maiden Goddess of Love, gave Mot a proper burial, and the crops grew again.

In this movie, Baal possesses a young woman who acts like a cat, then possesses Anthony Hopkins' character. Yet again, I'm slightly dubious about the amount of research done by the filmmakers. If they had learnt more about Baal, they may have seen him as a powerful prince, important enough to be referenced ninety times in Jewish scriptures, and as the deity in charge of the fertility of their fields—not as someone who gets a girl to purr and lick her bum.

THE DYBBUK FROM
THE POSSESSION

Also called dibbuk, and dybbukim when referring to it as plural, this is a fascinating spirit from Jewish mythology that, in this film, haunts an old wooden box.

The dybbuk is a spirit, usually of a nasty, malicious, not-very-nice person who possesses a person's body and soul. Because of this spirit's sins in life, its spirit wanders aimlessly around the world, trying to find a body to possess.

The term itself was created in the 17th century by German and Polish Jews, and is an abbreviation of the term dibbuk me-ru'ah, meaning cleavage of evil spirit, or min ha-hizonim, meaning dybbuk from the demonic side of man. It is linked to the term ibbur, the meaning of which has changed over time. If possession were a coin, ibbur would be the side that's in the light, and the dybbuk would be the side that's in the dark. An ibbur is a righteous spirit that occupies a person's soul for good, whilst a dybbuk possesses the soul with evil intentions.

The dybbuk can be seen in a painting by Ephraim Moses Lilien (1874-1925) who specialised in Jewish themes. Isaac Luria (1534-72) was another person to refer to the dybbuk—

Luria being a mystic who was thought to be the father of Kabbalah, a method of Jewish mysticism. He had a belief in the transmigration of souls, which is that a soul is reborn in successive bodies.

The earliest folklore indicated that the dybbuk would target a sick person, and would require an exorcism to be performed by a ba'al sham—the term for a miracle-working rabbi. Once exorcised, the dybbuk leaves through the small toe, leaving behind a bloody hole, and the spirit is either redeemed or sent to Hell.

In The Possession, a girl finds a dybbuk box, and unleashes the dybbuk that is found inside of it. This is said to have happened to a man called Kevin Mannis in 2001, who became a consultant on the film.

Bathsheba Sherman
from The Conjuring

This film is based loosely on The Haunting of Harrisville in 1971, a house where the Perrons lived between 1970-80. They were helped by renowned paranormal experts Ed and Lorraine Warren. The haunting is also discussed in a book called House of Darkness House of Light, written by Andrea Perron.

Although Bathsheba wasn't a demon, she was thought to be a wicked woman, and to many, a witch—even thought to be related to Mary Towne Eastey, who was burned for witchcraft in 1692.

She was born in 1812 as Bathsheba Thayer and later married Judson Sherman in Connecticut on March 10th 1844. She was a housewife, and her husband was a farmer, and she gave birth to her son, Herbert L. Sherman, in 1849 when she was 37. There are theories she had three other children who died before seven, though they remain unconfirmed.

One version of the story, which is contradicted by several sources, is that, in 1863, her husband caught her trying to sacrifice her son to the devil. Once caught, she climbed atop a tree, proclaimed her love for Satan, gave a curse to anyone who dared to use her land, and killed herself. This is why she is alleged to have haunted the Perrons and attempted to get the mother to kill her children.

The major flaw in this, however, is that the census has Bathsheba as dying in 1885, and has her son as living on to become a farmer.

The most trusted story is that a baby Bathsheba was looking after died in her care. It is said that this baby died because of a large sewing needle to its skull, but the courts didn't have enough evidence of her guilt to convict her.

This didn't stop the town's folk from seeing her as guilty, and the widely held belief was that she sacrificed this baby to the devil. They believed she was a witch and continued in this belief until the day she died of natural causes.

Valak from The Conjuring 2

Please don't confuse Valak with the Enfield poltergeist that the Warrens face in this story—there has been plenty written on the Enfield poltergeist, and you can even pay to stay in the house where the haunting took place.

Valak is the demon that haunts Lorraine Warren throughout this film, in the form of the nun and the crooked man—though the demon's mythology has nothing to do with nuns or crooked men. But we can be sure this was the demon the nun and crooked man represented in the film, as when Lorraine is confronted with the nun, there is an unmistakable whisper that leaves her lips of, "Valak..."

Valak is the 62nd demon in the Ars Goetia, said to govern 38 legions. He appears as a child with angel wings, riding a two-headed dragon. He gives answers on the location of hidden treasure and the location of serpents, whilst delivering them to the magician that conjured them.

Sounds good, but I still wouldn't recommend conjuring him. He controls a legion of serpents who do his bidding, and is said to be President of Jinnestan—the country of the jinn, a large sector in Hell, so the treasure probably isn't worth it.

The Pseudomonarchia Daemonum spells his name Valac, and also attests to him riding a two-headed dragon, whilst The Dictionnaire Infernal spells his name as Volac, and refers to him as a great president of the underworld. This text also states that, besides knowing the places of serpents, he also knows the position of the planets. A keen astrologer then, I guess?

Paimon from Hereditary

P aimon is the demon who arrives with two demons in tow—Labal and Abali, the latter of which is the demon used in *The Last Exorcist*.

He is the ninth spirit in the Ars Goetia, where he is described as a great king who is loyal to Lucifer, and commands 200 legions. He appears sitting on a camel with a crown on his head, and is introduced by a host of spirits playing instruments such as trumpets and cymbals. After the roar he always gives when summoned, he teaches arts and sciences, and he can provide the conjurer with answers to whatever question they ask—so make sure you have some good ones ready!

In fact, in some contexts, Paimon is not seen as evil, but as a teacher.

Then again, I remember quite a few teachers I had at school who were undoubtedly evil.

Before he fell from Heaven, he was an angel in charge of the order of dominations—meaning that he regulated the duties of the lower angels. As with any angel that God rejects, he simply didn't like that Paimon was questioning his methods and labelled Paimon as conceited, banishing him once he rebelled with Lucifer. Some sources also say he was one of the Cherubium—the angels who guard holy places, such as the Garden of Eden.

He is a prominent demon in the demonology texts, being granted quite a few mentions. The Pseudomonarchia Daemonum presents Paimon as a demon more obedient to Lucifer than any other, thrown out of Heaven for his arrogance and destruction. Once called, the conjurer will find him arriving from the northwest, full of answers to their questions.

In the Dictionnaire Infernal, his name is spelt Paymon, and appears on a camel, wearing a crown, but with a woman's face. Again, the text says he is good at answering questions. Perhaps I'll conjure him next time I need to know where I left my keys.

Paimon is also connected to the Tree of Death, which is an actual tree that exists in the Caribbean, Bahamas, and Gulf of Mexico. Its bark can leave chemical burns, and its fruit can cause vomiting and diarrhoea.

Basically, don't 'do an Eve.' Eating fruit off trees will either see you banished from paradise or have the shits—or worse, both!

The Mythology of Demons: Why so Different?

As we can see, so much of the mythology of demons is different, or inconsistent, from how the demon is portrayed in the film.

This leads to the question: why?

I find it unlikely that a filmmaker or writer will not have researched the demon they are using. But why is it, for example, that Pazuzu has no links to sex, yet is presented as a vile, sexually perverse creature in *The Exorcist*?

The answer is intrinsically linked with religion: demonic horror has deep roots with religion, and recent religions offer a black and white view of life.

For example, the ten commandments are finite instructions; they are rules, not laws. There is no leeway, or allowance, or understanding—they are dead-set commands that are, quite literally, set in stone. They tell you what you should or should not do, and offer nothing else.

"Thou shalt not kill" does not consider acts of self-defence, or war, or for a domestic abuse victim who snaps and kills her husband to protect her children.

"Honour thy father and mother" does not allow for

parents that are abusive or culpable of neglect. Should you honour a father who abuses you, whether emotionally, physically, or sexually? Absolutely not. But there is no room for manoeuvre; it is not flexible guidance; it is a *commandment*.

The Bible, like every other holy book, is full of instructions on how to deal with people and situations. Similarly, the Qur'an spends its second chapter telling, with no allowances, that those that "don't believe" will face "great punishment."

And so, for a demon to exist in horror fiction—or for someone to hold a belief in angels and demons at all, whether in the fictional realm of horror, or the fictional realm of religion—the belief requires a black and white view of good and evil. Angels are good, demons are evil, and that is the way of it. The demon represents Hell, all that is awful, everything that is perverse and evil—and its host, often a female child, is all that is pure and good.

The origin of Satan shows that there is grey between the black and white. Once, The Devil was one of God's angels—according to the books of Ezekiel and Isaiah in the Old Testament; he was one of the highest-ranking angels—but stood in defiance of God and began a revolt. Having failed this stand, Satan and his followers were condemned to hell. But why did Satan stand up to God?

There are many proposed answers to this question, but it depends on which way you look at it. In many religious stories, Satan wanted more power—he wanted to overthrow God so he could be the ruler. Of course, your view of an event can be changed through the lens you look at it, and there is another perspective—that Satan did not like the way God ruled. He saw God as a tyrannical dictator; one that did not listen, but commanded with an iron fist. If this is the case, we can liken God to dictators of history, such as Saddam Hussain, Joseph Stalin, or Kim Jong-un—and, if someone were to overthrow any of these dictators, we would celebrate them, and label them a hero. If this is the way you choose to see Satan's fall, then Satan is a hero who stood up for himself and the other angels that felt jaded by God's rule.

I imagine this theory will create anger in the most devout. That there are greys between the black and white of good vs evil is irrelevant to religion, and to demonic horror. We cannot know about Pazuzu's beneficial aspects in protecting the pregnant and the young, as that would ruin the illusion created by *The Exorcist* that good and evil are absolute.

Of course, any psychologist or psychoanalyst who has investigated crime and the reasons for people committing what we would deem 'evil acts' will probably tell you it's not as simple as that. All of us can be driven to commit evil acts. And my research has found that the demon is not necessarily representative of evil, but reflective of what one deems as evil at the time the religion, or the demonic horror book or film, was created; the demon represents what the male patriarchy of a society deems to be deviant behaviour. It is what society teaches us is evil.

For example, Regan's behaviour in *The Exorcist*, which is sexually vulgar and aggressive, is how the male patriarchy of 1970s America saw teenage girls. For the first time, teenagers were having a voice, and young women were sexually liberated. The contraceptive pill had been introduced, and women were more in control of their sexuality. Women could get divorced. Because of these changes, the male patriarchy saw these sexually open teenage girls and women as vile and vulgar—hence, why Regan, when possessed, is presented as such.

In fact, we can add to this that Regan was the daughter of a career-driven single mother, something that the male patriarchy would also have frowned upon—meaning that Regan is more likely to act in a deviant manner because of non-traditional parenting.

So who do they send to fix Regan? Two celibate priests!

Two men who have (supposedly) never had sex arrive to teach the sexually vulgar teenage girl how to behave.

It's also worth mentioning that, in the real life case *The Exorcist* is based on, the possessed victim was a boy. In the book and film, the sexually perverse actions were better suited to a girl.

The Entity was released in the 1980s, first as a book, then a movie. It is about a woman who is raped by an invisible entity, and the police and psychiatrists don't believe her; they would rather think she's crazy than believe that she's being molested. In the book, she ends up being driven crazy in a mental institute, her condition undoubtedly exacerbated by those who disbelieve her. In the film, she just comes to terms with being raped by this entity as there is nothing she can do about it.

I'm not sure we can find a better metaphor for the experience of a rape victim. Whilst we still hold a prejudice in society, whereby a rape victim is often not believed or is re-traumatised through their attacker's trial, it was even worse in the 1980s. Sentences for rape were ridiculously low, and women were frequently believed to be hysterical rather than believable.

In *The Entity*, the rapist is invisible because that's how it feels for the rape victim; that the victim is the only one who can see the damage being done, and it causes everyone else to doubt her. In the book, the re-traumatisation of talking about the experience to professionals who disbelieve her makes her go crazy, whilst in the film, she simply must accept rape as a part of her life as no one else will do anything about it.

In *The Entity*, we see the male patriarchy's views of the 1980s reflected. The victim was a single mother with three children, desperately trying to maintain a financial situation that allowed her to keep the small house she had. Perhaps it is no coincidence that she is seen as hysterical and is not believed. Every male character she meets wants to protect her; the professionals and ex-husbands feel they need to teach her about life. She is constantly patronised by men who have the view of a woman being a delicate creature who needs nurturing and protecting.

Ultimately, in demonic horror, the demon is something evil, and the host is something good and pure—even if that evil represents deviant behaviour and the good represents the innocent victim. And, in this way, demonic horror highlights the damage of this black and white view religion preaches. Every word of a holy book is about how one should live their life, rather than the intricacies of the human condition that lie beneath our actions. There are reasons someone becomes a criminal, or even a killer—and they usually have nothing to do with them being 'evil.'

We need to provoke thought, not tell people how to live. People behave better when they understand the reason behind why they should act a certain way.

Of course, I am sure that there are many priests, vicars, imams, pujaris, and spiritual healers that give speeches and sermons aimed at conjuring thought. They might ask questions intended to make you think—but they will also have an answer the questions are intended to direct you to, e.g., 'God is loving.'

We require better teachers than that.

We require teachers who allow us to develop and explore our own perspectives, not guides who direct us through leading questions toward an already prescribed requirement of behaviour.

So where does one look for such a thing?

I have the perfect suggestion...

An Alternative to Religion: Shakespeare and Philosophy

There are two things I detested as a child—religion and Shakespeare. Probably because they were both shoved down my throat throughout school. With only one of these, however, have I changed my mind.

At primary school, we were forced to sing hymns in assembly, followed by a prayer, and even at a young age, my scepticism made me wish not to take part. Was this allowed? Was I, as a child, allowed the freedom to decide not to pray or sing hymns?

No. They gave me detention for refusing to follow their religious practices. Meanwhile, I had severe mental health issues, and my parents were desperately beseeching the school to help in looking into them. The school refused. I wasn't diagnosed with a mental health issue until seventeen, at which point my adolescence had already been taken away from me.

For me, it is not the notion of God that I have a problem with; rather, it is religion itself.

I do not mean for you to mistake me as an agnostic, I am definitely an atheist—I do not believe there is a god. Too many times I hear the argument "but science can't explain everything!" To which I reply—that doesn't mean that the answer is automatically God; it just means we don't know. But, even though I don't believe in it as a concept, I don't take issue with it. It is religion that poisons the concept.

The god a person believes in will almost always be decided, not by the truth of which is the true god, but by the god that they were taught to believe in, whether by culture, family, or circumstance. For example, if you grew up in the Middle East, you'd probably be Muslim. If you grew up in the white middle class of England, you'd probably be Christian. If you were alive 3000 years ago you may have been Zoroastrian—a religion that featured virgin births and a horned lord of darkness far before Christianity stole their ideas. Alternatively, if you'd have been born in the Akkadian Empire, you'd have been part of the Sumerian religion that worshipped An, Enlil, and Enki. And if you were alive 2000 years ago, you might be Pagan—as this was just before the Catholics slaughtered the Pagans to ensure they were the prominent religion.

In fact, so many acts of genocide have been committed by Catholics over the past two millennia, that the reason you might be Catholic is not because Catholicism is correct, but because thousands to millions of people have died to ensure you are more likely to become Catholic now.

Let's take an example. Cathar was a huge religion in the twelfth and thirteenth century. But why are you unlikely to meet a Cathar today? Because Catholics wiped them out to ensure they remained the dominant religion of the time. So the reason you might be Catholic instead of Cathar now is not because Catholicism is correct, but because Catholics murdered enough Cathars in 1209 to prevent the likelihood of you becoming a Cathar above Catholic. In fact, only the Black Death killed more people than Catholics in this period of history.

And, of course, in referencing how the circumstance of

your birth decides your religion, I am not just referring to Islamism, denominations of Christianity, Hinduism, Buddhism, Paganism, or whichever religion one might follow. I also refer to the religions that have died out: Zoroastrianism, Vedism, Tengriism, Ashurism, Manichaeism, Atenism, Mithraism, or any of the other religions you probably haven't heard of, simply because it is not the prominent religion of the time and culture you happened to be born into.

But my dislike of religious institutions isn't simply because of the flimsy nature of their foundations, but because of some of the horrific things they say in their holy books.

Read Deuteronomy or Leviticus from the Bible and you will read some of the most awful ideas anyone could think of. Seriously, even Donald Trump sounds nice compared to these books.

Let's take a few examples:

> *"When a woman has a discharge, if her*
> *discharge in her body is blood, she shall*
> *continue in her menstrual impurity for*
> *seven days; and whoever touches her shall be*
> *unclean until evening" (Leviticus 15: 19-20)*

So are Christians meant to see a woman on her period as disgusting? No wonder there's such discomfort around men discussing menstruation.

> *"You may purchase male or female slaves from*
> *among the foreigners" (Leviticus 25:44-46)*

This sounds like you are allowed to take foreigners from abroad and make them your slaves. Do you remember when this happened? Yeah, it wasn't good.

> *"If a man meets a virgin who is not betrothed,*
> *and seizes her and lies with her, and they*
> *are found, then the man who lay with her*
> *shall give the father of the young woman*
> *fifty shekels of silver, and she shall be his*
> *wife" (Deuteronomy 22:28-29)*

I'm often criticised by theists for quoting the Bible, and am often met with the response that "it's meant to be metaphoric, so stop taking it so literally." Tell me, please, what is metaphorical about the guidance that when a man rapes a woman, he must subsequently pay her father to marry her?

Of course, Christianity is not the only holy book with such disgusting lessons, but this is not a chapter dedicated to ranting about holy books. No, this is a chapter that offers an alternative to a holy book.

For when one is an atheist, where does one look for life lessons? We are not born with an intrinsic belief in right and wrong; these are concepts that are taught to us by society. So where do we go to explore life when religious teachings fail us?

This is where we turn to literature. There are many authors we could turn to, to help us learn about life: George Orwell, H. P. Lovecraft, Charles Dickens—hell, even J. K. Rowling. In this circumstance, however, I am discussing Shakespeare—the other concept that was rammed down my throat as a child.

I honestly believe that education is the reason for destroying a child's love of reading. As an English teacher, I am made to teach multiple texts, only one of which can be modern. And by modern, that often means post 1960—and I do not class a book published in 1961 as modern.

This means that education often leads students into believing that books are old, stuffy, over-descriptive novels, as one would find in classical literature. No wonder our younger generations aren't reading enough. A teenage boy doesn't care about *Pride and Prejudice*, just as they won't show interest in *Wuthering Heights*. So why not let them learn about a book that's more exciting—that will make them want to keep reading?

I was forced to read Shakespeare on multiple occasions during my education, and when you're a child, it's an alien language. Reading is already challenging enough when you're learning how to do it, so why then force a child to read lots of words that won't make sense to them, and that they will never have to use again in their life?

It took years until I looked at Shakespeare again; when I was forced to because I had to teach it. I dreaded the thought of teaching Shakespeare, but ended up loving it, and soon realised that the problem wasn't with Shakespeare, but with the way it is often taught. I really enjoy finding ways of bringing *Macbeth* alive for my students. My students' faces when I explain what "he unseemed him from the nave to the chops" means are priceless. The play is violent and gory, and in finally understanding it, I can learn to appreciate it.

And, in learning to appreciate it, I can finally see the value in the quotes and concepts that Shakespeare gave us. There are so many elements of his plays, whether it is a simple line or a theme that explores an ethical conundrum, that can help us learn about life, ourselves, and the world. We can respond to situations with our own perspective and explore the character's reactions as a way of evaluating our own ethics.

As Dumbledore once said, words are "our most inexhaustible source of magic."

But don't just take my word for it—let's look at a few examples, beginning with *Macbeth*.

At the beginning of the play, Macbeth is told by a group of witches that he will become king. He tells his wife, and she gets consumed by the idea, which subsequently puts in motion a series of events that results in Macbeth becoming king. The line of thought this poses presents quite the paradox: Macbeth killed the king to become the king because of a prophecy that he would become king; but if the witches had not given him this prophecy, he would not have killed the king, and so he would (probably) not have become king.

So this begs the question: What is the burden attached to knowledge? Do we carry out our actions based on the expectation of the response those actions will provoke? Does the expectation that we will achieve something make it more likely – for example, if we truly believe we will win the football match we are playing in tomorrow, does that belief therefore make it likelier to happen?

And does the burden of knowledge create the evil that it provokes? Macbeth was a loyal companion to King Duncan, being one of his most trusted warriors, and one of his closest friends. The knowledge that he *could* become king drove him to kill that man who loved him. The witches—which, at the time of Shakespeare, would have been a shocking and grotesque thing to have on stage—tempted him into evil by verbalising their prediction. Did they just give this prophecy to see if Macbeth would follow through on it? Does this show the fallibility of man as much as it shows man's desperate need for power?

And let's not forget the role of Lady Macbeth. It is her who manipulates her husband into killing the king, and it is this character that explores femininity and gender. For example, when she is willing herself to do what must be done to remove King Duncan from his throne, she says, "unsex me here." She wishes to remove all feminine traits and become masculine, as this will make her more ruthless. Does this work? Is it simply the belief in gender roles that makes her more ruthless, and if you removed belief in gender roles, would women be just as ruthless as men?

And is she not ruthless in the way she manipulates

Macbeth? She manipulates Macbeth by claiming that, upon his request, she would rip a baby she was breastfeeding away from her nipple and kill it; she is *that* faithful to him. She creates such violent imagery when she is making no attempt to be masculine—so does that mean it is only the belief in masculinity being more violent than femininity that makes it so? Then again, is her manipulative nature seen as a feminine characteristic? And, if it is, is this an accurate representation of femininity? Or is it all based on the construction of gender roles as created by society?

You can see that, through just a few references to Macbeth, we are already asking questions that people should be asking. In today's society, the desperation for power, the expectation of immediate gratification, and what gender roles mean and should be, are all pertinent questions. *Macbeth* draws our attention to them in a way no religious book does.

One might claim this is because the plays are more modern than religious texts that are evidently outdated—but let's not forget, these plays are five hundred years old. Yet, unlike religious texts that still dictate our actions based on the belief of people who lived thousands of years ago, the themes and questions of Shakespeare are timeless. For example, religious texts were written when we had the belief that God was in charge of the weather and would reward us with sun—a belief that even most modern religious folk consider to be outdated—yet it is still a recurring theme in the lessons of the Bible, insinuating that people who turn to the Bible for guidance seek advice that does not apply to our current knowledge.

(For examples of references in the Bible to God controlling the weather, see "when He thunders, the waters in the heavens are turmoil, and He causes the clouds to rise from the ends of the earth" in Jeremiah 10:13, and "He unleashes His lightning beneath the whole heaven and sends it to the ends of the earth" in Job 37:3).

Shakespeare, however, despite being written in a time where belief in witchcraft was rife, gravity was undiscovered, and the theory of evolution was not yet proposed, still wrote plays that posed questions about human nature that are still relevant today.

Let's look at *Hamlet*, another of Shakespeare's most prominent plays. It is the story of a man whose uncle kills his father to marry his mother and take the crown. I know, right? Sounds like the kind of thing you'd get on Jerry Springer. Unlike The Springer Show, however, *Hamlet* does not have a bunch of obese rednecks fighting each other—what you have is an elegantly brutal exploration of madness and heroism, and the paradox of being both heroically mad, and neither mad nor heroic at the same time.

Much like many horror texts, such as *The Turning of the Screw* and *A Head Full of Ghosts*, we are unsure whether or not one of our central characters is mad. Hamlet sees his father's ghost, who tells him of his murder, and so acts like he's a lunatic to stop others from realising that he is conjuring a perfect plan to overthrow the man who murdered his father. But, considering he believes he has seen a ghost, to what lengths is his madness real? Is it just the belief of the audience that the ghost was real that makes him not mad? Is the assessment of whether someone is mad subject to our beliefs or prejudices?

The play explores the difference between appearance and reality: the presentation of the man who isn't mad, but presents himself to be so, against the king who is mad, but presents himself to be rational. Perhaps we are quick to judge one's image without delving deeper into their reality.

The nature of revenge and justice are explored, and the difference between the two is examined. Should Hamlet take revenge on his uncle? If he does, is it revenge, or is it justice prevailing through ensuring that the man who bears the crown is deserving of it? And what of honour—is defending your father honourable, and is murdering your uncle honourable? When is it honourable to take vengeance or implement justice? These are questions our politicians should ask when deciding which countries to invade, considering the amount of mess our countries have made when invading societies we deem to be 'less advanced.'

As well as posing several themes that prompt debate and discussion, there are many quotes in *Hamlet* that are worth further examination:

"There is nothing either good or bad but thinking makes it so." Does good or bad exist, or does something become good or bad when common thought suggests that said thing is good or bad?

"The body is with the king, but the king is not with the body." Only the king, in his own body, can ensure his rules are enforced—but doesn't that mean one should still obey his rules when he is not there to enforce them? Are society's rules there to be obeyed only when someone is watching? Is it the principle we should obey, or the fear of being caught?

And, of course, the most famous Shakespeare quote of all —"To be or not to be, that is the question." It is a question many who suffer from depression have asked: What is most preferable, life or death? Does one end suffering associated with life with the belief that life is more suffering than pleasure, or does one hold on with the belief that pleasure will arrive in time?

Finally, we can't mention Shakespeare without mentioning *Romeo and Juliet*. This is seen as an epic, romantic story, but it's not. It's about a seventeen-year-old and fourteen-year-old who meet, fall in love, and kill themselves five days later. The kids could do with getting a grip, but youthful infatuation is what it is. But, alas, the romance might not be exactly what the story is about.

The story is about the feud between two families, the Montagues and the Capulets. Several murders are committed because of this feud, and the destruction will continue to occur as the families pass the feud onto their children. They do not directly murder Romeo and Juliet, but their hatred causes their deaths.

We can liken this feud to many feuds we see today, such as when a family falls out, and the destruction that occurs for the rest of the family; or when a marriage falls apart, and the effects of conflict on the children. But, perhaps most pertinent, is the likeness to the feud between countries, or religious sects of the world.

Over 100,000 civilians died in the Gulf War (source: forces.net).

Al Qaeda saw this, as well as other events, as part of the west's attack on Islamism. In response, they took 2,996 civilian lives in the tragic events of 9/11.

The Americans reacted by declaring a war on terrorism and, as a result, the British and Americans were so desperate to remove Saddam Hussain that their forces took 12,152 Iraqi civilian lives in just the first year of the 2003 war on Iraq. This was more than four times as many deaths as in 9/11 (source: iraqbodycount.org).

And so it continues.

One side attacks, then so does the other.

It seems like it's been this way for a long, long time. In fact, we can go back to the crusades between 1095 and 1291, when Christians slaughtered Muslims to take back what they deemed holy land. Nearly a millennium on, the fighting continues, and no one has learned any lessons. Much like the Montagues and the Capulets, the hatred has left nothing but destruction in its wake. Destruction of lives, homes, cultures, and societies.

And children of the opposite sides who attempt to be

friends (or lovers in the case of Romeo and Juliet) are prevented from doing so, and progress cannot be made.

It is religious extremism that inspired the beliefs that drove these wars and attacks. Whilst many will preach that religion teaches love, it is too often used for hatred.

Shakespeare has never been used to incite an attack, but it has been used to promote ethics, debate, and thought for any who choose to use it. Perhaps we should look at such literature to guide us, and to teach us right from wrong, rather than outdated holy books that can bring out the best in some, and the very worst in others.

It is also worth noting, as this chapter ends, that it does not need to be Shakespeare. His plays won't resonate with everyone. But there will always be literature that will encourage you to explore moral conundrums with an open mind, allowing you to witness different sides of an argument and develop a greater understanding of the human condition.

If you wish to keep an element of spirituality, I would recommend *The Five People You Meet in Heaven* by Mitch Albom. It is a story about a man who dies and meets five people in the afterlife who he once knew, each of which played a pivotal role in his life. It teaches us that we affect others without realising it. That every little, insignificant moment of contact can be a huge moment in another person's life.

The Harry Potter series explores what it is to be good or evil. How one should treat their enemy. How one should try to save someone who appears bad. The difference between the good and evil characters in J. K. Rowling's stories is that the evil characters judge, with prejudice, those who they do not consider to be a pure race of wizard—whilst those who are good allow room for change in those that are evil. When Malfoy repeatedly cannot kill Dumbledore in *Harry Potter and the Half-Blood Prince*, Dumbledore does not shout or condemn, but offers help—saying that he once knew a boy "who made all the wrong decisions." In a moment where Dumbledore could lose his life, he tries to help a wayward teenager, rather than condemning him as evil for his actions.

And, of course, horror, whilst often violent and absurd, mirrors society without the boundaries of other genres. We explore socially unacceptable behaviour, what is right and wrong, and what is good and evil.

It is in my atheism that I have found strength, and in literature than I have explored life. Many people who are religious could not understand how atheism possibly helps someone in the way religion has helped them. In the following chapter, I will attempt to explain how, whilst a theist might believe that religion adds value to life, I believe there are other ways to find value.

Being a Happy Atheist

When it comes to discussions about religion, I find it hard not to voice my dislike. I do not write this with the intention of offending, but this is a book of my thoughts, and it is difficult for me not to share my disdain.

If my thoughts cause offence, then I would also ask you to question why you are offended. I am simply voicing the opposite opinion. It is odd that it should cause such a volatile reaction for me to do so.

We live in a society where, if someone says, "I know there is a god, you'd have to be foolish to think otherwise," there is no reaction.

But, if I was to say, "I know there is not a god, and you'd have to be foolish to think there is," then HOLY MOLY just look at the response I receive. This sentence has caused me to be labelled aggressive, insensitive, difficult, and nasty. For me, there is no difference between these two sentences. So why is it some religious people get more defensive?

It is because it is far easier to pick apart and destroy theist beliefs than it is to pick apart and destroy atheist beliefs. I believe that this is a reaction to the ease at which an atheist will put forth the most rational arguments in a debate, and the anger this causes in those who, if they were to question their beliefs, would have to question the perspective they have held for their entire life.

This causes what is known as cognitive dissonance—the psychological reaction that occurs when someone is shown evidence that contradicts their opinion and, instead of considering the strength of the evidence, forces them to cement their original belief further in defiance of the evidence. Even if you offer incontrovertible evidence, thoroughly reasoned and researched arguments, and perfectly articulated points, it creates dissonance—a sense of anxiety—that means that person's belief will become stronger in the face of opposition. It is more likely that a theist would read this chapter, be offended, and believe what they believe more strongly.

This is why such lively debates are often killed with the simple sentence: "It's just a matter of faith."

This sentence requires the least amount of intelligent thought to put forward. It is the least rational and the most irritating of responses—because when that is your response to every argument put forth, where is the discussion meant to go?

Christianity is based on books about a prophet called Jesus.

People began writing these books almost a century after Jesus was supposed to be alive.

They each have different accounts of the same events, making the perspectives questionable.

They were written at a time where beliefs that someone can walk on water would be valid, whereas now such beliefs would be delusions that would be seen as part of psychosis.

There are many books that have been eliminated from the Bible, that have since been discovered. For example, Judas's book was found—but was not translated for decades after its discovery because of Christian denial that it was valid.

The Bible has been translated so many times that it's become a game of Chinese Whispers. If you read some of the analysis of the original words, you'll see how different the interpretations were before the King James version—yet many Christians still swear by what is written in the King James version as if it is sacrament.

The Old Testament requires a belief that the Earth started 5,000 years ago. We know this is not true. Why do we not understand that the knowledge is outdated? Why are people so uncomfortable with just saying, "I don't know how it all began"? Because, honestly, we don't. We just don't.

It is also worth pointing out that any new religions that have emerged, such as Scientology, have been labelled cults—but when you look at the origins of that religion/cult, it bears great resemblance to the foundations of religions we accept as religions because they have been around for much longer.

But the response to this compelling evidence is: "It's just a matter of faith." What is one meant to do with that?

Another inevitable response I hear is, "Well science can't explain everything"—which is an excellent point, and one that I wish would apply to religion too!

Yes, science can't explain everything. But lack of explanation is not evidence for God. It simply means we do not know.

And we need to become more comfortable as a society with saying, "I do not know."

"But what of the comfort that religion brings?" is the next question. And this brings me to the crux of this chapter.

In my response, I will direct you to a brilliant quote from Douglas Adams, where he says that one does not need to believe there are fairies in their garden to see that it is beautiful.

It is human nature to always want more than you have, but here is the greatest life lesson I have ever learned:

Happiness is based on expectation.

My ex-girlfriend really wanted to buy a house. It was all she craved. She went on about it for years, struggling to save every month for a deposit. Then we bought a house, and a week later, she was miserable again. Because she came to expect to have that house, therefore it stopped making her happy.

Once we get what we crave, we come to expect it, therefore it becomes an expectation, and ceases to make us happy.

If you have a nice house, you'll want a bigger one. If you get the job you want, you'll eventually want a promotion. If you have enough money to buy food, you'll want enough money to buy nicer food.

The same happens with drugs—the more alcohol you have, the more you then crave. Religion is a drug. If this world isn't enough to make one happy, then one needs to create a god to give it meaning. Whatever a person has, they will need something more to make them happy. The solution is not to keep craving more: it is to learn to appreciate what you have; stop expecting to have it, then you will find out how magnificent all you have is.

And this is the drive behind a belief in God. You come to expect this wonderful world we have, and once it becomes an expectation, you need something more to make you happy— you need to believe in God, as the world is no longer enough.

What do I suggest as an alternative?

Instead of having to believe that heaven exists to comfort you about the thought of death, be grateful for the existence you've been given in the first place. The odds of you being alive are so astronomically small that just to be alive for the time you are given is miraculous. Heaven was invented to bring comfort, when having had life in the first place should be enough to make you realise just how fortunate you are.

So instead of looking at your garden and wishing it was bigger, look at it and appreciate that it could be smaller. That some people don't even have a garden.

Instead of needing a god to make life valuable, look at the value your life already has.

If you spent a year living with half of what you currently have—half the money, half the house, half the family, half the love—then, once you regain what you currently have, you will feel a lot more grateful for it, and you will no longer crave more.

Many rich people are still miserable. They have what so many others crave, but it clearly doesn't make them cease craving more.

The key to happiness is not to imagine there is more to give your life meaning. It is to stop craving that extra thing you think you need to give your life meaning; it is in looking at what you have and being happy for it.

Instead of needing a god to give your life purpose, see the purpose that is already there. Look at the brilliance in your life that you don't give enough credit to.

The truth is, life is meaningless. There is no purpose to us existing. We are one of many billions of creatures that have existed on this planet—a planet that is probably one of many, many more.

But this isn't a depressing thought—it's a liberating one. It means that you don't have to keep searching for the meaning that isn't there. It means that you can provide your own life with its meaning, instead of relying on something else to do so.

As the philosopher Albert Camus said, it is in revolt that we find meaning. It is not in the meaningless of life, but in the defiance of that meaninglessness that we find our meaning.

If we can give our lives their own meaning—whether that

is to love, to write, to raise children, to help others, to spread kindness—then we can find a much greater purpose than devotion to a deity of dubious origins.

Finally, I wish to comment on the concept of open-mindedness. It is a common occurrence that, in a religious debate, when I say, "I do not think there is a god," I am frequently given the accusation that I need to be "more open-minded." But this makes little sense to me.

After all, a religious person will say, "God is the answer," and the line of thought ends. They will give this as their conclusion; that there is a god, and the god is as one's religion dictates it to be. Whereas, to my mind, there are thousands, possibly millions of possibilities to our origin. I am open to many, many possibilities, God being just one of them (albeit an unlikely one), that explains how we got to where we are—but the religious perspective provides only one option.

Now, please tell me how, when I am the one open to many, many possibilities, and religion is only open to one, it is that I am the one that is not open-minded?

I considered whether to leave this chapter in, knowing the reaction it would likely receive. I am expecting to get several negative customer reviews on Amazon by religious readers who are angered by my opinion, rather than open to it. I would expect nothing less from the internet. But at least we have a name for what it's called—cognitive dissonance—and a reason many people stubbornly refuse to adapt their beliefs to current knowledge.

After all, most people who have religious beliefs have had it since childhood. It is usually a belief that is indoctrinated in children, subtly forced on someone from a young age—and it is immensely difficult to undo damage done in childhood. We all suffer from trauma we've experienced at a young age, and once someone has something engrained in their beliefs for so long, it takes a lot to change it.

I will leave the subject of religion having conveyed my opinion, hoping that you have gained a valuable insight into the mind of an atheist. We do not believe that there is nothing to live for—quite the contrary; we find everything to live for, as we provide that meaning ourselves.

Shortly, I will return to horror, and the question of how it is created—but first, let's look at what the purpose of demons is in religion, and why they were created.

Because, let's be clear—they were created, not discovered.

So what was the purpose of religion creating such a thing?

Demons as a Tool for Control

Throughout history, religion has provided comfort and strength to those who follow it.

Or has it?

In today's society, we have laws, rules, and values that govern the way we live. We have police to enforce them. But the police didn't exist until the mid-1800s. Those in charge needed other ways to control society and ensure that people followed their rules.

That is why the Old Testament, if you read it thoroughly, is pretty much just a big book of rules—most of which are actually quite worrying if you read them.

But surely you could have chosen not to be a religious person, and be an atheist?

Eeehh. Actually, no.

To do so would have risked abandonment. Or death. Or worse, torture. You might have your breasts chopped off. Or have been executed. Or burnt to death.

Not being religious really wasn't an option.

Religion was conditioned into the general population since

birth, and people grew up fearing the morbid consequences of not following their religious teachings.

This meant that religion was the perfect way to ensure cooperation. And this is evidenced by some instructions given in the Bible which, when you read them by today's standards, are actually pretty horrific—but give a very clear indication of what the standards and expectations of older societies were.

Here are a few examples:

> *But I say to you, That whosoever looketh on a woman to lust after her hath committed adultery with her already in his heart (Matthew 5:28)*

> *If two men are fighting and the wife of one of them comes to rescue her husband from his assailant, and she reaches out and seizes him by his private parts, you shall cut off her hand. Show her no pity. (Deuteronomy 25:11-1)*

> *When a man sells his daughter as a slave, she will not be freed at the end of six years as the men are. If she does not please the man who bought her, he may allow her to be bought back again. (Exodus 21: 7-8)*

> *If a man happens to meet in a town a virgin*
> *pledged to be married and he sleeps with her,*
> *you shall take both of them to the gate of that*
> *town and stone them to death—the girl*
> *because she was in a town and did not scream*
> *for help, and the man because he violated*
> *another man's wife. (Deuteronomy 22:23-24)*

The first ensures that no man ever commits adultery by ensuring that he is in fear of even looking at another woman.

The second ensures that if a woman tries to intervene to defend their husband, and in doing so goes near the man's privates, she will lose her hands.

The third ensures that even a female slave does not have the rights of a male slave—and that if her slavery does not please her owner, they will buy her again, thus enforcing the inferior view of women.

And finally, probably the most horrific one—if a man rapes a woman, and that woman doesn't scream loud enough for help, they should stone her to death.

Before you ask, yes, these are genuine quotes from the Bible, a book that many people throughout the world swear on, then get defensive when you question them on it.

These are lessons used to control people in society back when it was the most powerful tool those in charge had. Without police around to impose laws like we have now, having religious texts that specify guidance on adultery, slavery, rape, and many other topics ensures that society kept people in check.

It's not just in Christianity, either. Why do many Muslim women wear a hijab? Many Muslim women I've met say they do it by choice, but how do you define 'choice'? If it's a value they've been taught to obey since they were child, then is it a choice that they follow it as an adult having been conditioned into it?

If a woman needs to cover her hair because a man finds it sexual, that is the man's problem. The man needs to control himself. A woman should not have to dress modestly to ensure she doesn't attract unwanted male attention, or because men can't control themselves around her. We live in a society where, when a woman gets sexually abused, the attention often turns to what she was wearing, or how she was acting, rather than to the behaviour of the man who committed the abuse—when you teach women they need to cover their hair to remain modest, you teach them that a man's attention is her fault, not the man's responsibility.

It also contributes to a larger value that is often embedded within Islam—the place of women. It is part of a teaching that ensures women do not risk any sexual liberty, such as pre-marital sex, and that they do not question the dynamic of a marriage where the man is in control.

But what was it the religions of centuries ago feared? Why did they not dare go against the values instilled by their religion?

They feared the consequences of God's unhappiness, or the consequences of allowing The Devil's wrath to enter their lives through sin.

And this is where demons come in.

Each demon was created as a tool for control. It ensured that people lived in fear of behaving in an unwanted way.

Take Belphegor, for example—a demon who originated in Hebrew lore in the Kabbalist tradition and was later adopted into Christianity. He is mentioned in The Dictionnaire Infernal as "a demon of discoveries and ingenious inventions"

—but, most significantly, he is known to take "a young woman's body."

In the Treatise of Confessions by Evildoers and Witches, written by a German theologist called Peter Binsfeld in 1589, Binsfeld uses the seven deadly sins as a basis for classifying demons. For example, Lucifer represents pride and Leviathan represents envy. In this interpretation, Belphegor represented sloth. The demon represented negligence and apathy. According to Thomas Aquinas (an Italian Dominican friar and priest in the 1200s), sloth inspires all the sins that arise from ignorance.

Imagine it's the 1600s, and you have a town of people who aren't harvesting crops fast enough, who aren't working to the speed at which those in charge wish them to. Introduce Belphegor. Show them what happens to the lazy. See how quickly they get on with work with that threat hanging over them.

But demons aren't always used for a single purpose. They can be used to threaten people about what might happen because of more than one unwanted behaviour. That is why Belphegor also has links to sexual liberty.

The demon was said to emerge from Hell in desire of sex, wishing to experience the pleasures of sex—however, he found sex to be so awful that he retreated to Hell, desperate to be somewhere in which an act such as sexual intercourse did not exist.

Adding to this the interpretation that Belphegor can also appear as a sexy young woman to tempt men, he is quite a threat to those who wish to pursue an affair out of marriage, or those who see sex as something other than the act of procreation. In a society where sexual repression was essential, and enjoyment of sex was seen as negative, this demon was crucial in reinforcing both this interpretation of sex, and the possibility that, should one sleep around and seek sex for pleasure, they might end up sleeping with an abominable demon by accident.

In Histoire Admirable de la Possession et Conversion D'Une Penitente (known in English as Admirable History)—a grimoire written by a French inquisitor called Sebastian Michaelis in 1613—Michaelis comes up with one of many classifications of demons that have been written over the past five or six hundred years. In this classification, there are many demons that serve a similar purpose to Belphegor.

In his first hierarchy of demons, there is Asmodeus, who tempts men into wantonness; Berith, who tempts men into murder and blasphemy; Astorath, who tempts men to be lazy; and Gressil, who tempts men with impurity, as well as others. In the second hierarchy, there are several more demons, such as Carnivale, who tempts men into shamelessness, and Oeillet, who tempts men to break the vow of poverty.

These are all standards that society in the 1600s wished to enforce, and these demons ensured people obeyed under the threat of the demonic. It might seem laughable nowadays that people would live their lives based on fear of demons a few people seemed to randomly come up with (people who would mostly be considered mentally ill in today's world) – but you need to consider the society of the 1600s. There was no knowledge of evolution, of gravity, of a round world; there was no knowledge to challenge religion. Religion was the only possibility, and it ruled people's lives as they believed demons could bring famine, death to their crops, and harrowing punishment for their sins, just as they believed God might send thunder when he was angry. Therefore, demons were as much of a threat to them as a mugger or murderer might be to us when walking alone down a dark alley at three in the morning.

People would avoid wantonness if Astorath was the threat that hung over them, avoid impurity as the threat of Gressil was more powerful than any devotion to their spouse, and avoid blasphemy when Berith might respond.

Particularly noticeable is how Oeillet tempts men to break a vow of poverty—which isn't a vow people often take nowadays, thus showing how much these demons were a product of the time. Nuns, monks and some priests might have taken a vow of poverty as part of their religious orders, and this demon would try to make them turn back on their religion—the ultimate sin of the time.

It is truly a fascinating aspect of demonology to study. The creation of each of these demons reflects the world in which they were believed to be present, telling us so much about the beliefs and expectations of the time and place of their invention.

And now, out of sheer curiosity, I am going to look at The Satanic Bible, and ask whether it is a book of evil, or whether it is simply an alternative way of looking at things.

SATANISM: IS IT ALL THAT BAD?

I can almost feel the controversy created by the title of this chapter.

Maybe you've flicked through the pages of this book upon its arrival, or swiped through the contents on your Kindle, and you saw this chapter, and you thought—*what the actual fuck?* Hey, I wouldn't blame you. Satanism hasn't had the best reputation over the years.

So, with the knowledge you have, I can imagine this chapter title will have an obvious answer:

Yes, Rick. Yes, it is. Satanism is really that bad.

But if there is one thing that I wish to achieve in the 'philosophy' part of this book on *Horror, Demons and Philosophy*, is to have you challenge all those societal norms that have been taught to you since the day you were born. This does not necessarily mean entertaining Satanism as an option, but gaining better knowledge about what you wish to argue against.

For example, I have read a lot of the Bible. I have read a lot of the Qur'an. For me to be an atheist who speaks about the negative effects of these religious books, I need to have actually read some of them.

So let me ask you, ye who sits there automatically saying Satanism is awful—have you actually read The Satanic Bible?

I will assume, based on statistical presumption, that you have not.

In which case, the only evidence you have to back up your argument is that you have been taught that Satanism is bad.

If God is good, then Satan is evil, then that means it's bad.

However, further analysis highlights how it isn't as simple as that.

I have already quoted Bible verses in previous chapters, so I won't do that now—but it's quite clear upon any reading of the Old Testament that the Christian God is not a loving, forgiving force. He demands sacrifices; he demands prayer—and he created people so that they can worship him. Within the scriptures, he condones murder, encourages slavery, and condones rape. In fact, God's kill count in the Bible is 2,038,344, whilst Satan's is 10 (source: Wired.com). God is actually, when you think about it, a bit of a prick.

We have also seen, in the 'true' mythology of demons that I have previously outlined in this book, that the background of demons aren't as simple as 'they are bad, so they were sent to Hell.' In fact, many of the demons simply questioned the way God did things, so God banished them for questioning him. We wouldn't accept our government doing this, yet we accept it in our God.

In fact, The Devil himself was cast out of Heaven because he disagreed with God. Many stories of his banishment do not tell of evil acts—instead, they speak of how Satan did not believe God was all-powerful, and that he didn't like the way God did things, so he tried to stand up to God, and God banished him for it.

Imagine working for a boss who, when you try to offer an

idea of a better way to do things, not only fires you, but sends you to the pits of Hell. Would you want to work for that boss?

It's also true that the concept of good and evil is a matter of perspective. Very rarely does someone who's committed evil acts actually believe they are evil. And, whilst religion teaches a black and white view of right and wrong, I would suggest that right and wrong exist on a spectrum.

Not everything is as simple as good and bad. Imagine a man who steals from you. He's done something bad. Now, discover that he's a drug addict because his dad kicked him out at thirteen. He spent a few weeks in a foster home where he was abused. He's been living on the streets ever since. So, although his action was bad, is it really that simple?

So, to return to the aforementioned statement: *If God is good, and Satan is evil, then that means Satan's bad.* We've learnt that God has not always been a good guy; that Satan could have, from one point of view, been standing up for what he believed in; and that not everything fits neatly into the categories of absolute good and absolute bad.

Therefore, we must conclude that in teaching us such a statement, society is incorrect.

So we return to Satanism. Is it as simple as we've been led to believe? Or is it simply an alternative point of view to the religious dogma that doesn't appear so innocent on further inspection?

The stories we've heard about Satanists are pretty bad. Most reports of Satanism come from a time of panic toward cults following the Manson murders in the 1970s—something that is reflected in horror novels of the time, many of which were based around cults.

Richard Ramirez, a US serial killer in the 1980s who'd break into people's homes during the night, showed a Satanist symbol on the palm of his hand during his trial.

In the 1970s, Sean Sellers had shown his devotion to

Satanism by carrying a vial of blood around his neck. He killed his stepfather, mother, and a shop clerk who wouldn't sell him beer.

More recently, and this time in the UK, Danyal Hussein was sentenced to life in 2020 for murdering two women as a sacrifice to a demon who would, in turn, allow him to win the lottery.

This seems pretty horrific, and some might say conclusive. Then again, are such examples of extremism not found in all major religions?

In fact, we will find far, far, far, far, far more murders committed throughout history in the name of God than in the name of Satan, many of these acts of genocide, many of them committed by Catholics intending to ensure the domination of their religion, or to protect perceived holy land.

Similarly, I know that Al Qaeda are Muslim, but I know with absolute certainty violent Islamic extremists are in the huge minority of Muslims.

So can we not apply this logic to examples of Satanism? If there's one thing we've learned about the human species, it's that they will find any excuse they can to kill others—and religion is often that excuse.

I think it's wise to point out at this stage that I am not a Satanist, and that I am not endorsing Satanism, just as I would not endorse Catholicism.

But I also find it interesting that I have the urge to tell you this.

Why, when investigating this topic, do I need to keep reminding you that I'm simply asking questions, not taking a side?

It's because of stigma. It's because everything we know as humans is based on our biases and our limited experiences. I believe what I believe because it is the belief created by my life experiences—whether this is by my actions, treatment by others, societal messages, constant reinforcement, or whatever other subtle elements may have affected my subconscious without ever even knowing about it.

But, although I am no exception to this, *I know* I am no exception to this—and this is important to recognise, as it helps us to maintain an open mind; it is crucial that we challenge the perceptions that we are taught.

For that reason, I bought a copy of *The Satanic Bible*, as written by Anton Szandor LaVey, and published in 1969. And, after a brief reading of a few dozen pages, I have two reactions.

First, that some of it offers a better, more natural alternative to the abstinent, constrained life proposed by religion.

But only some of it.

My second reaction is that, if Christianity is one extreme of the belief, comprising an abstinent, constrained life, then this Satanic Bible is the complete other extreme, offering natural chaos.

To highlight this, I will share with you the 'nine satanic statements'—the guidelines that I assume are offered as an alternative to the ten commandments—and my reaction to them.

1/ *Satan represents indulgence instead of abstinence.*

I am undoubtedly against abstinence. I think holding back your natural impulses, so long as they do not harm others, makes no sense. We were given them for a reason.

At the same time, I don't think extreme indulgence is necessarily beneficial, either.

For example, to be abstinent and refrain from sex before marriage is to deny the biggest drive nature has given us. Sexual exploration is a part of finding yourself, and youthful investigation allows you to learn what you like and how to have a better sex life. Abstinence removes pleasure for no reason other than for the sake of not having pleasure.

However, I am sceptical about the benefits of overindulgence in this situation either. Not to say that there is no problem with behaving in a way that society views as promiscuous—society's expectations be damned! If you are doing this for the enjoyment and pleasure of it, then go ahead. But whilst there are some who enjoy a full sexual life, there are some that use sex to gain self-esteem. It acts as a rush that provides a temporary bout of improved self-image, but when this dies down, one will have to seek another sexual partner to experience it once more. In this way, indulgence is just as harmful as abstinence.

Perhaps moderation would be the better suggestion.

2/ *SATAN REPRESENTS VITAL EXISTENCE, INSTEAD OF SPIRITUAL PIPE DREAMS!*

This suggests that we should focus on what is happening now, instead of making up concepts such as heaven.

Whilst they dressed this statement in a particularly harsh linguistical manner, I relate to the meaning. When I am grieving a lost loved one and someone tells me, "It's okay, they are in heaven", I find it really hard not to lash out. Not only are they assuming my beliefs, they are making up lies to make the truth better.

When someone I love dies, I do not make up an afterlife to comfort myself. Instead, I reflect on the life they've lived and relish in the opportunity they had to live it. It is such a slight chance that we even exist in the first place, and however little time we have, it is a blessing. We should not need to make up magical ideas to make magical what is already so very wonderful, and I understand the sentiment of what is being said here.

3/ *SATAN REPRESENTS UNDEFILED WISDOM, INSTEAD OF HYPOCRITICAL SELF-DECEIT.*

Again, this seems like quite a harsh way of describing religion, but one I understand.

Rather than deceiving ourselves that someone is guiding us, we should seek wisdom elsewhere. Once you detach yourself from the notion that someone else is responsible for guiding you, you can take responsibility for your own life and seek life lessons in other places.

4/ *SATAN REPRESENTS KINDNESS TO THOSE WHO DESERVE IT, INSTEAD OF LOVE WASTED ON INGRATES.*

This seems quite similar to the statement by Jesus during his Sermon on the Mount: "do unto others as they do to you."

I am hesitant to agree with either.

Perhaps we should not waste our kindness on people who are not willing to be kind in return—but this seems to suggest that we have a limited supply of kindness and must choose carefully who to spend it on.

Sometimes, showing kindness when it's hardest to show it, is truly divine behaviour.

Say a man barges you off the bus, tells you to "fuck off", then falls over. He wasn't kind to you, so why should you be kind to him and help him up?

I will tell you why: his wife could have just died. Or he could be struggling to maintain his relationship with his children. Or he might be losing his job. He is close to breaking, and he doesn't know how much more he can take.

Your act of kindness in this situation might change this man's life.

Yes, he was nasty, but you don't know what's going on in his life. Helping him up and smiling at him despite what he's done is a rare behaviour, but is behaviour that could make an enormous difference to this person.

5/ SATAN REPRESENTS VENGEANCE, INSTEAD OF TURNING THE OTHER CHEEK.

Again, this is similar to what the Bible preaches.

I can hear religious folk reacting angrily to this, claiming that religion preaches turning the other cheek. In which case, I would direct you to the famous Bible quote in Leviticus 24:19-21, which says, "And if a man cause a blemish in his neighbour; as he hath done, so shall it be done to him; breach for breach, eye for eye, tooth for tooth: as he hath caused a blemish in a man, so shall it be done to him again."

I would also refer you to the Qur'an, verse 16:26, "If you take revenge, then do so only in proportion to the wrong done to you."

It seems that there is little difference between Satanism and other religions in its advocating vengeance.

6/ SATAN REPRESENTS RESPONSIBILITY TO THE RESPONSIBLE INSTEAD OF CONCERN FOR PSYCHIC VAMPIRES!

I'm assuming "psychic vampires" is meant sarcastically. It suggests someone who is omnipotent and all powerful, whilst also suggesting someone that manipulates you.

Does this mean we do not show concern for those who are manipulative? Or does it mean we stop blaming God for man's awful actions?

I'm slightly unclear about this one. It is starting to feel more and more like these statements are poking fun at, religion. I hoped for helpful alternatives rather than a war between the two.

7/ *SATAN REPRESENTS MAN AS JUST ANOTHER ANIMAL, SOMETIMES BETTER, MORE OFTEN WORSE THAN THOSE THAT WALK ON ALL-FOURS, WHO, BECAUSE OF HIS "DIVINE SPIRITUAL AND INTELLECTUAL DEVELOPMENT," HAS BECOME THE MOST VICIOUS ANIMAL OF ALL.*

I love this one.

Freud's theory of dreams highlights how he believes dreams are our mind's way of working through what we repress to fit in with society. For me, this is another reason why we love horror—it allows us to explore what we repress.

While many of Freud's theories have been torn apart in the last century, I wholeheartedly agree with the idea that we have animal impulses that we frequently deny.

In his book, *The Murderer Next Door*, David M. Buss discusses how it is natural for humans to have homicidal fantasies, and that most of us have had one. Similarly, many studies have proven that humans are not naturally monogamous—that monogamy is something we must force on ourselves.

But what happens to this rage when someone upsets us? To the evolutionary psychology of murder? To the sexual urges you have when choosing to be monogamous?

As a society, we'd rather convince ourselves that these things don't exist. Instead, we think of ourselves as a better species than other animals, and religion reinforces this.

This is truly where the human race shows just how arrogant it is; to be convinced that we are better because we believe ourselves to have a higher level of intelligence. Truth is, dinosaurs were around for millions of years as the dominant species and never caused the problems to Earth that we have in less than a century.

The world has existed for 4.543 billion years. Yet, our species has been around for 200,000 years, civilisation has existed for roughly 5,000 years, and it has taken less than that to drive our planet to the precarious position it's in now.

Within decades, we have invented technology that sends poisonous gases into the air, have almost destroyed our climate, and have caused global warming.

In years, we have almost destroyed a planet that has been fine for billions of years.

Yet we insist we are a better species?

Just look at what we have done.

We are the worst species, and are made even worse by our belief that we are superior.

8/ SATAN REPRESENTS ALL OF THE SO-CALLED SINS, AS THEY ALL LEAD TO PHYSICAL, MENTAL, OR EMOTIONAL GRATIFICATION.

I would agree that the seven deadly sins are another example of religion's unhelpful view of the world as black and white. To condemn certain emotions, such as lust, envy, or greed, as sinful is unhelpful. If we are to have a healthy mind, we need to allow ourselves to feel our emotions without guilt; to process them, and to understand what's made us feel that way. If we are envious, why do we feel such a way?

At the same time, indulging in something for the gratification of it without considering the consequences to others is also unhelpful. If your greed is at the expense of the less fortunate, but you do it because it leads to gratification, then that is not okay.

9/ *SATAN HAS BEEN THE BEST FRIEND THE CHURCH HAS EVER HAD, AS HE HAS KEPT IT IN BUSINESS ALL THESE YEARS.*

The final statement is slightly unhelpful.

I appreciate that it's highlighting that religion has controlled its populous through fear for as long as it has existed – but this is an attack, rather than an act of guidance.

And it is in this that I lead to my conclusions about Satanism.

It seems that it is no better or worse than any other religion.

Every religion attacks other religions. It's been going on for a long, long time. I'm not sure how this is any different.

I was hoping for an alternative that puts us in touch with our true impulses. Whilst it certainly does that, it takes it to the extreme, and it phrases its beliefs as an attack on other religions without intelligent debate to back it up. Just as religions condemn other religions for taking false gods or prophets, this one has phrased its guidance as a mickey-take dripping in resentment.

I am aware this may seem hypocritical, as I cannot stop my resentment toward religion from coming through in my writing, but at least I am offering alternatives or backing up my statements. These are just angry remarks dressed as statements about how we should act not just as nature intended, but in the volatile way nature intended.

But, whilst I have found no epiphanies in Satanism, I have found nothing new either. I will let religions continue to argue it out whilst I pop a good horror film on.

It's the best kind of indulgence, after all.

And now, for the final few chapters, we are going to leave demons and satanism—I have discussed them, as well as philosophy, a great deal. For now, I am going to look at horror and the creation of it.

The Zombie Phenomenon

Zombies, the phenomenon that originated in Haiti folklore a few hundred years ago, has since become a western obsession—yet it often divides horror fans.

When I wrote a zombie trilogy, half of my readers were keen for my take on a genre they love, and the other half were less enthused, finding zombies to be a silly concept.

I must admit that I am in the pro-zombie squad—I love a good zombie film. From George A. Romero's *Night of the Living Dead* film that inspired five sequels, to the trashy rehashes, to the modern interpretations—I love them.

More recently, we have moved away from the slow-moving zombie. Many auteurs still choose to keep the classic sluggish creatures, such as the hugely successful *The Walking Dead* series and the highly entertaining zombie musical, *Anna and the Apocalypse.* As much as I adore them, I must admit that I find the faster zombies far scarier. Netflix's *Black Summer* has created a terrifying zombie—any person who dies will be a zombie within seconds, and they will sprint at their victim. You need a horde of zombies for them to be scary in many of the classic, slow-moving zombie interpretations—but you only need one to terrify you in *Black Summer*.

Zombie films pose a fascinating psychoanalytical question. When we watch a well-made zombie movie, we will be tense, on edge, and often scared of the zombies. But zombies don't exist in our reality, so why are we scared of them if they are not a real-life potential threat?

It is in this question that we must explore what the zombies represent. Even though zombies aren't real (or are they?—more on this in a bit), there are so many threats about a zombie that exist in our reality. It could be a fear of being bitten, of being chased, or of what others become. It could be the potential quest for survival when there are no police, army or government—it highlights to us just how helpless we are without societal constructs to keep us safe. You cannot reason with a zombie, just as you cannot reason with a psychotic serial killer—it is a threat that will be a threat until it's destroyed.

All horror reflects society and often highlights its darker side. All art is a perspective of the world it comes from, but horror is a genre that does this without barriers. For example, in the 1950s and 60s, American horror was all about alien threats attacking its characters, whilst 80s American horror is about the threat from inside; about the evil that lurks within the perfect suburban image. This is the difference between the post-war fear of attack versus the fear of Regan's government and the destruction of morals from within. And this is where zombies really come into their own—zombie movies are excellent at providing a political allegory, or a reflection of philosophical musings that our society struggles to confront.

George A. Romero created his *Night of the Living Dead* series with the intention of providing a political commentary. *Night of the Living Dead* is about the working class and racial tensions, with an African American lead at a time of changing attitudes toward ethnic minorities. *Dawn of the Living Dead* is about capitalist consumerism; all the zombies gravitate toward the shopping mall as it's what they are used to, perhaps suggesting that we are all mindless zombies going to the shopping centre to spend money as a capitalist society requires us to. *Day of the Dead* showed the enemy (zombies) learning how to attack the characters better at a time of cold war tensions.

Whilst these political messages were intentional, I wouldn't say all horror auteurs intentionally place reflections of society in their work. But, whether intentional or not, it must be impossible not to show the world that you live in through what you create. With this in mind, I wish to highlight more recent zombie films, books, and television series that have explored societal tensions and have posed interesting questions.

The Walking Dead has been a hugely successful franchise, becoming one of the most watched programs on television. Described as a soap opera during a zombie apocalypse, it frequently poses questions that compromise the ethics we believe we hold. For example, in season two, Rick must choose whether to let a boy live, knowing that the boy might lead the rest of his group back to the farm where Rick and his pregnant wife live, or whether to take the boy's life in order to eradicate the possibility.

This may seem like a far-off conundrum, but it is not. Whilst it may not involve killing a boy, we are constantly evaluating conundrums by consciously or unconsciously analysing the odds. Our governments are frequently deciding whether to go to war based on similar circumstances. They are choosing what they believe will keep us safe—or, conspiratorially, what will help society prosper through wealth or oil.

Witnessing such problematic situations in the fictional world forces us to question what we would do in that situation. Whilst most of us would claim we'd let the boy live, the television show highlights that we make such hypothetical assertions whilst watching in the safety of our homes, not having to face the fatal consequences of such a tough decision. When it comes to protecting our family and ourselves, how much risk would we really be willing to take?

Similarly, *World War Z* highlights the potential consequences of a government's poor decisions. In real life, we invaded Iraq under the pretence that Saddam Hussain had weapons of mass destruction, and he didn't. We invaded Afghanistan, started a war that wouldn't end, then left only for the Taliban to reclaim it, leaving many to think that the deaths of many British and American troops were lost in vain. Our governments make stupid decisions over and over—or, if you agree with the wars, let's say that they execute their decisions poorly. Each time, it costs lives.

Let's just look at the pandemic—whilst many countries were preparing for lockdown, Boris Johnson did not attend meetings about the pandemic, and allowed the Cheltenham races to go ahead. In the US, Donald Trump was so stupid he encouraged people to protest against state-enforced lockdowns. These decisions cost lives, and the average person has had to pay for it.

World War Z sees a government fail to act, and fail to manage a worldwide catastrophe, and sees many die as a result.

I mentioned *28 Days Later* earlier in the book, and how, during animal testing on monkeys, a group of scientists inject a rage virus, which leads to country-wide destruction. What does this suggest about what many people feel about scientific testing on animals? And what of the ethical implications of the experiments many scientists perform that involve messing with nature—should we be doing it, and what might happen if we continue?

Later in the film, the army offers shelter to the survivors, then decides to rape their women. Surely this reflects how many people feel about those that are supposed to protect us?

Particularly women, who, for example, turn to police when they are abused, only to find themselves re-traumatised when their abuser goes to court. Perhaps it represents the high number of people who are in positions of care who have abused those who trusted them to take care of them. Catholic priests, charitable entertainers, film producers, teachers, doctors—many roles that come with a duty of care have seen examples of people who've abused their positions. Horror, as ever, has highlighted that darker side of our society.

Yet, even among horror fans, there are some who refuse to watch zombie films because of the ridiculous concept of zombies. But now I will pose the question—how ridiculous is it?

I will not assert that zombies are a certainty, or that they are an imminent possibility—but that something that is akin to a zombie could happen.

But how on earth could zombies happen?

I have a few suggestions....

Rabies is a virus that spreads through the saliva in animals. Although very rare in humans, it is a virus that spreads through dogs, bats, coyotes, and other smaller animals. It infects the brain and the nerves, and can cause aggressive behaviour. Similarly, mad cow disease destroys a cow's brain and spinal cord, and can induce psychotic behaviour.

How possible is it that a similar virus might pose a threat to humans? Would this not create a zombie-like state?

What is even more convincing, however, is the concept of a parasite that might work on humans—and, when you think about it, this is actually quite possible, and quite scary.

A parasite is a small creature without a brain that controls another animal. It is quite amazing how something that does not have a brain itself can control the behaviour of something far bigger. Let's look at a few examples.

Ophiocordyceps unilateralis fungus is a parasite that

controls ants. It attaches itself to the spores, then attaches itself to the skeleton, then takes over the body. It makes the ant leave its group and seek an area where the temperature is ideal for the parasite to reproduce. It then forces the ant to attach itself to a leaf while it dies.

Leucochloridium is a parasite that invades a snail's eyestalks. The parasite needs to be in a bird's belly for the best conditions to reproduce, so it controls the snail, forcing it to go into the open so a bird can eat it, thus allowing the parasite to reproduce in the bird's guts and release its eggs into the bird's faeces.

Think that parasites only exist in small animals like snails and ants? Think again! Angiostrongylis cantonensis is a parasite that infects a rat, as well as snails and slugs. What's more, the parasite can end up in a human when ingested through uncooked snails, or from water or vegetables that have been contaminated.

Each of these parasites controls its host, forcing them to leave its social group, and seek the best conditions for it to reproduce, which usually means fatal repercussions for the host.

How unlikely do you really think it is that a parasite might one day evolve to infect humans and control their behaviour?

I mean, I know I've already said it, but a parasite doesn't even have a brain—they don't need to be that powerful to control a host. How much evolving do they really need to do to control a human?

And what if that parasite needed a dead human to reproduce? Might they be able to control their host enough to kill the nearest human so that the parasite might pass into the corpse's body? Might that not look quite similar to a zombie with the rage virus as seen in *28 Days Later*?

Sure, it might seem like a far-off concept—but didn't a worldwide pandemic seem far-off in 2019?

For now, I do not live in fear that such a thing would happen, but I am fascinated by the possibility. If such a parasite could breed and spread quickly, it could easily overtake us as the dominant species on this planet. In fact, Athena Atkipis of Arizona State University has claimed that more than half of the species that exist on Earth are already parasites (source: phys.org).

Either way, maybe we ought to get our zombie survival kits ready, just in case...

Approaches to Writing Horror

In his book, *The Secret History of the World*, Jonathan Black makes many ridiculous arguments about philosophy—namely that we should go back to the way we thought about the world thousands of years ago, which would inevitably mean dismissing the accumulated knowledge of the past few thousand years and its impact on the way we currently look at the world.

Black highlights how the human species used to look at the world in the lens of mind-over-matter, whereas now we look at the world in matter-over-mind. We used to think about things in terms of how they affected us spiritually, whereas now we analyse how things actually are. Whilst now we look at atoms and matter and analyse how they work, back then we emphasised what we saw and how we felt about whatever the atoms and matter took the form of.

Once I moved on from how much his frequent claims of spirituality over science annoyed me, and I looked for some modicum of value in Black's book, I realised how crucial this concept is for the creative writer, and especially the horror writer.

Black has a point about how important it is to explore our own perception of the matter that makes up the world, and not just place emphasis on what the world consists of. However, rather than explore this in the spiritual sense as I believed he was advising, I think it's an important process of thought in understanding how you view the world, what various objects and events mean to you, and what your biases are. And it is here where great writing becomes excellent writing.

If I were to describe a monster with the mindset of matter-over-mind, I might describe how it had big, bulging eyes, or grotesque skin, or a distinct and disgusting aroma. I would describe the matter that makes up the monster. I would tell the reader what the monster *is*. Whilst it is important that the reader knows what kind of monster it is, it is nowhere near as important as knowing how your character is *experiencing* that monster, for that is when you truly bring that monster to life.

So, if I were to describe with a mind-over-matter thought process, then instead of describing how the matter gathers together to create the monster, I would describe how the matter that makes up the monster is processed through the mind of the character perceiving it.

I might describe the way the coarse feel of the monster's scales makes the character's fingers twitch and prick. I might describe how the foul aroma of the monster makes the character choke and feel nauseous. I might describe how its big, bulging eyes make the character feel like his entire body is being examined, and I might describe how all of this makes his knees quiver, his heart race, and prompts thoughts of what he would have said to his wife that morning knowing he was probably about to die.

Through emphasising the process of the mind that perceives the monster rather than just the monster itself, you bring it to life. You provide the reader with the experience of the monster, rather than a simple gimmick.

This, of course, leads to the question—must a horror story have a monster?

I must confess that I struggle to think of a horror book or film without a monster. However, I use monster as a loose term. It could be a literal creature that attacks the protagonists, or it could be what a person becomes, or it could even be an abstract concept.

Take *Cabin Fever*, for example. A group of teenagers stay in a cabin together as a deadly sickness spreads among them. In terms of a literal creature that attacks them—no, there is not one. There is nothing lurking in the woods about to attack. However, perhaps the presence of the monster could be in what the characters become. They shun those who are sick, even locking one in the shed and neglecting her. Perhaps the monster is an abstract concept represented as the sickness.

The monster is simply one of the ingredients that makes up a good horror story.

Cabin Fever is also a typical example of a group of people who go to a cabin in the woods. We also find this in *Evil Dead*, *The Strangers, Funny Games, Deliverance, I Spit on Your Grave, Eden Lake, Misery, Wrong Turn*, and the aptly named *Cabin in the Woods*. Even if it isn't a cabin, we often see characters stranded in the middle of nowhere, such as in *House on Haunted Hill, Night of the Living Dead, Rec*, and much of the *Saw* franchise.

Why is this such a common trope of horror, you ask?

Because it is part of another vital ingredient of a good horror story: isolation. The characters must be cut off in some way from those who can help. Although this doesn't, as my examples suggest, have to be in the middle of nowhere. Take *Panic Room*, for example—they are in a house between plenty of other houses, but they are stranded for most of the film in the panic room, afraid of their home invaders.

Many horror writers nowadays bemoan the presence of mobile phones. In the seventies and eighties, horror writers could trap a character somewhere with no way out, whilst nowadays a trapped character can just pick up their mobile phone and call the police. This often leads to the weary "oh no, I don't have signal" copout.

But that misses the point.

Not only must the characters be isolated, there must also be something that compels them to stay in the isolated, perilous situation; often in a link to the story.

For example, imagine the character can call the police, or can get in his car and drive away from the isolated cabin. However, his home invaders have his daughter trapped, and are threatening to kill her if he calls the police. Here is an example of someone who is staying in the isolated environment because he is compelled to.

What if one of the home invaders is someone the protagonist loves?

What if the protagonist is convinced that the ghost might either be her dead husband, or might be stopping the dead husband from coming through?

What if their son is inside a zombie infested house, and whilst they could run away, they can't leave their son?

These are all things that tie the narrative to the character, which is crucial. Whilst the concept of a story might convince someone to read or watch it, it is the characters that will make someone invest in that story. If the character has no ties to the conflict, or can simply leave the situation by having phone signal, then you are missing a trick—you are not making the story personal enough for the character.

Whether your story's selling point is the concept, the monster, or the situation, it's all about how the characters respond to it. They guide our empathy and fear, and too many bad horror films get this wrong.

Not that the story isn't also important, but it is not as important as the character's experience of that story.

Usually, a horror story will start with a situation. In *Misery*, a crazed stalker traps an author in their house. In *The Exorcist*, a mother realises her daughter is possessed. In my novel *Psycho B*tches*, all the women in the world turn into feral zombies. It is then up to you to take this situation, insert great characters, give them a reason to care, and let them go from there.

There is often a requirement of horror that there is a large build-up, but this isn't always appreciated. If you read any debate in any horror group on Facebook, half of the horror fans will say they appreciate a slow burn, whilst the other half will say it gets boring.

Personally, I'm starting to dislike slow burns. I read a lot of horror books, and when I must read 200 pages of each horror book until something exciting happens, I get bored. I can only read so many slow burns.

Of course, there are exceptions. Sometimes the characters will be so interesting that I want to hang out with them. Although it's not horror, I felt this way with *Girl on a Train*. This isn't something a writer can always anticipate, however, as we all have different taste in people and characters. Even so, whilst your character doesn't have to be likeable, they should be interesting enough to keep us going through the build-up.

In terms of slow burns, however, I propose an alternative. A compromise between the two. Take time to build up and let us get to know the characters—but make things happen at the same time. Even if it's just witnessing other characters being chased by the killer, or an alternative timeline that shows big events that inform the current story.

I did this with a few of my books. With the entirety of *The*

Sensitives series, an eight-book series of paranormal horror novels I published, I'd have a current timeline that I introduced with the word 'NOW.' Whenever I would feel that not enough was happening in the build-up, I would then insert a 'THEN' scene. It wouldn't just be interjected for the sake of it, of course, and it would always have some relevance to the story. Perhaps I'd introduced a new character in the 'NOW' storyline, such as Father Connor O'Neil in *Questions for the Devil*, and I wished to tell more of their story within this non-linear narrative via the 'THEN' storyline. I'd reveal bits of information about his story that would alter how the reader perceived the current narrative of the story. In the end, he turned out to be a different person than who the reader initially thought he was.

Another example is my book, *Shutter House*. This was more of a slasher story. I wanted to introduce the character of Amber and her brothers and show their reason for being compelled to enter the killer's house, but wanted to provide something to maintain the reader's interest in the meantime. As a result, I inserted a few scenes of the killer murdering some of his victims as I built up the characters and their conflict.

We live in a society where people's attention spans are growing shorter. When I was a child, I'd have to wait for an entire week until the next episode of *Buffy the Vampire Slayer* was aired, and months until the next series premiered and allowed me to watch the conclusion of the previous series' cliff hanger.

Nowadays, you can go onto Netflix or Amazon Prime and watch the entire series in one. You don't have to wait anymore.

We have technology that supplies us with immediate gratification. No more endless debates in the pub—you can find the answer to a question on your phone. Social media provides hits of dopamine that one would not get nearly as often a few decades ago.

Younger audiences are becoming older audiences, and soon they will be the entire audience. There is no attention span for slow burns anymore.

I may be wrong, but I can see it becoming more and more important to keep inserting these hooks into stories to maintain the interest of the reader whilst the story builds up.

But even without this emerging dilemma, why not give your reader as much titillation as possible? It is what horror is for, surely? Not to just wait for something to happen whilst we get to know the characters, but to be horrified and disgusted and frightened and amazed as much as possible.

So give me great characters, let me see the horror through their eyes, and give me as much of that horror as possible.

Don't hold back—it's horror. I'm reading your story because I want the thrills of an exciting genre.

Leave the yawns to the period dramas and give me something nasty!

Life As a Horror Author

I wasn't originally planning on becoming a horror author. My first book was a crime book called *The Art of Murder*. I remember sending it to a developmental editor, and the first thing they said in their feedback was, "well done for writing a book." When that's their first comment, you know the book is awful.

Still, I took on their feedback, and the book received some positive responses. It was, however, full of grammar errors and was formatted incorrectly. A year or so later, when I knew what I was doing, I paid for professional copy editing and bought software that would format it correctly. I also unpublished the original sequel I wrote for this book as it was awful.

I remained resilient, though, and it occurred to me—why am I trying to write crime? Horror is my true love. I should write that.

And so I did. I published *The Edward King Series,* starting with *I Have the Sight*. Reading it now makes me cringe—my ability to craft prose has improved a lot. Still, it continues to get a great response, which I imagine is more about the story I created. Even though I was still yet to perfect my ability to use language, my ability to craft a story has always been strong.

The next book I wrote that wasn't part of this series was called *The Understudy*. You won't find it anywhere, as I unpublished it. Even so, this is probably the most important book I've ever published.

No one ever learns by getting things right. You might achieve success, but you will not develop your craft. As Conor McGregor once noted—"Either I win, or I learn." Many people get something wrong and decide they are not good enough, and this is not the correct attitude to take—it means you have the opportunity to develop, and this is what I did in this instance.

Everything about *The Understudy* was wrong. The way I dealt with the subject matter, the prose, the editing, the story, the style—everything was awful, and my customer reviews made this absolutely clear.

Back then, when I first started, I would read my customer reviews every day. A positive one would make me smile, and a negative one would crush me. Nowadays, I don't read them— though my family does, and will often let me know if there is a particularly nice one. I have grown a thick skin now, however. If you look at the customer reviews for *Girl on a Train,* or *Harry Potter,* or *Gone Girl*—all fantastic books—you will still find scathing reviews, often with a personal attack on the author. The internet seems to make people with nasty opinions think their opinions are valid. We all get them, but these reviews are simply a testament to how you can't please every- one, and you shouldn't try to. Back when I first started, however, I hadn't gained this perspective, and some reviews hurt. I wondered whether I was actually good enough.

But success isn't the lack of failure—it is the conquering of it. I learnt from my mistakes, and my books became better as a result. That is why *The Understudy* was my most important book—every book I've written since has been better because of it. It was what I needed to take my writing to the next level. Without this experience, I probably wouldn't have been able to give up my day job within two years of publishing my first book.

For *The Edward King Series* and *The Sensitives*, I wished to include real demon mythology, so I thoroughly researched the demons I used. Sometimes, I'd use my creative freedom to adapt the demons, but, generally, I was quite faithful to the demon's background.

(If you wish to learn more about the demons I used and their background, I have already discussed this in my book *The Demonologist Handbook*—which you can get for free by signing up to my mailing list on rickwoodwriter.com)

For my post-apocalyptic Cia Rose series, I wanted to use my imagination. I invented four new creatures, each an adaption of an existing species:

- Masketes were an adaption of birds, with an almost tetradactyl-like quality.
- Thorals were large, four-legged creatures.
- Liskers were like giant snakes.
- Wasters were people who had sold their souls and their consciousness in return for survival, agreeing to be slaves to the monsters, becoming cannibals not too dissimilar to zombies.

Of course, as any good writer knows, whilst it is the idea/concept that might sell your book, it is the characters that make people engage with the idea. Having grown tired of the typical female characters I kept reading, especially in horror—normally weak, in need of being protected, or simply serving as the love interest—I wished to write a kickass female character who protects other people instead of needing to be protected

—which is where Boy came in. Boy is an autistic teenager that Cia grows to love and protect.

As I stated in the chapter *The Real Monster*, I believe horror is at its best when it asks the question: who is the real monster? And I wrote *When the World Has Ended* (originally entitled *After the Devil Has Won*) to keep asking that question.

Yes, we have the four monsters I've stated—but they are animals acting on instinct. Meanwhile, humans continually act in monstrous ways, even though they should know better: Cia's father abandons her to save himself; Cia is taken in by a group of survivors who just want to use her to reproduce; and survivors saved by the government study the creatures through torturous methods.

Perhaps the biggest question of who the real monster is, however, comes at the end of the novel. I don't want to give away what happens in case you haven't read it, but Cia's actions have divided readers of the book distinctly into those who approve of what she does and those who do not.

Of course, Cia's actions could seem monstrous—but you undoubtedly understand why she does them, which is perhaps the point of what she does: Once you understand why someone evil does an evil act, they cease to become evil, and we progress as a society.

It is, of course, the *Blood Splatter Books* series that I have prioritised in the past year. Whilst my other series feature continual story lines, this series was designed to be a group of standalones. I loved *Goosebumps* books as a child—they used to be 3 for 2 at WHSmith's, and my mum would always buy me some when we went into town. As a teenager, I progressed to *Point Horror*. I wished to create a series of standalone horror books for adults.

I decided each book would be a splatter punk novel—a term given to trashy extreme horror novels of the 70s and 80s. I made the covers to look like old horror movie posters that have been worn down. And, whilst each novel is violent and nasty, they all have an observation on society. I try not to shove the rhetoric down the throat of the reader too much, however, as enjoyment of the book should be the priority—the only book I feel I may have slightly prioritised the message was *Psycho B*tches*.

On the face of it, this book appears hugely sexist. Not just in the title, but in the cover that features a demented woman, and the concept: that all women go crazy and attack men. This is intentional, however, as I wanted to mislead the reader—it is actually a feminist novel that comments on everyday sexism by inverting such actions against men.

Ironically, I run a Facebook advertisement for this book then has the headline: 'All women have gone mental', and barely a week goes by without a man thinking they are original and hilarious (which they truly are not) by commenting on the advert, saying something like 'they already are', or 'they must be on their period.'

That these blokes actually think this is a joke no one else has thought of shows just how much the message of this book is needed. The reason that these men don't see how many other men have commented on such things, is because I routinely check the comments on the advert and delete any such sexist comments.

I did a lot of research into subtle pieces of everyday sexism and tried to show them happening the other way around. For example, in the novel, a woman goes on a chat show with her husband. The host discusses her role in her latest film in more depth, then turns to the man and asks what he's wearing to the film's premier—showing the difference in the kinds of questions male and female celebrities are asked. Also, this female character gives a lot to charity, then turns into a clever, conniving predator when her true colours are revealed—in what was a parody on abusers who get away with their actions due to the power or status they hold.

Similarly, the main male character is told by his mother that the shorts he's wearing make him look like a slut, and the male character is hesitant to go out at night for fear of how a woman might hurt him. There are also male characters grooming other men for one of the 'zombie women' they keep in the bedroom.

I came across a harsh review of this book online by a woman who stated that it was as if I was 'mansplaining feminism.' Whilst I get her point, it frustrates me. If we wish to eradicate everyday sexism, then we need men to educate other men—we need men to use their platform, such as being an author, to highlight such issues. That review didn't encourage me to continue standing up for such causes, and I think the person who wrote it should consider what effect she has on someone trying to help the cause.

Honestly, I think I did a better job of exploring sexism in my novel *Sex Blood*. It is about a woman who has an STI that doesn't affect women, but makes men's penises explode. Through this bizarre concept, I explore rape culture and the way men behave toward women. For example, as men are afraid catching this STI, they do not wish to attract unwanted female attention. They watch what they wear and go to nightclubs in large groups for protection, much as many women feel they must do in reality to protect themselves from unwanted male attention. I was proud of this book—I feel this book was stronger in conveying the complexities of these issues.

I have used other *Blood Splatter Books* to make observations about society. *Home Invasion* features a poor man robbing a richer man, and is a statement on privilege. *Haunted House* highlights domestic abuse that occurred during Covid lockdown, and how many victims were trapped inside with their abusers. *Shutter House* and *This Book is Full of Bodies* are about how it is easier to get away with evil deeds when you're rich.

Woman Scorned is, perhaps, one novel that lacks the same message as others. It is a rape and revenge novel, and for that reason, I was hesitant to write it.

Rape and revenge films are usually about a woman, often from the city, who goes to the country and gets raped by a group of men and left for dead in the first half of the film. She then takes her revenge on them through murder and torture in the second half. They are seen by some as empowering women, but probably seen by most as hugely sexist and demeaning toward women. Often, the first half that features the rape is the focus of the titillation, and is glorified more than the revenge element.

So, when I sat down to write my rape and revenge novel, I tried to think of ways that I could avoid falling into the same traps. Some may argue I failed. Some may argue I succeeded. Some may be undecided—which is probably where I sit.

The novel features a couple instead of a single woman. The most graphic rape scene is not against the woman, but is against the man, who is murdered first. The woman then escapes and returns to avenge her husband. This is where I tried to make it different—so many revenge plots feature the woman being murdered, and a man feeling the need to avenge her. Instead, I made the man the focus of the 'titillation' in the first half, and the woman as the one who takes revenge, not just for what happened to her, but for the man that she loved.

Perhaps this is where the message lies in *Woman Scorned*. That it is not a man's responsibility to save a woman, and that a woman is just as capable as sticking up for her man.

I have several ideas for upcoming *Blood Splatter Books*. I hope to cover as many subgenres of horror as possible, and to do it in the most entertaining, violent of ways—whilst also considering the deeper subtext.

First and foremost, however, they are for enjoyment, both for me writing it and for the people reading it. As academics, we are constantly looking for hidden meanings. As auteurs, many authors and filmmakers are always trying to peddle messages in their work. That's fine, but I think it's important that we make entertaining our audience the priority, not the message. It is most important that you find pleasure in what you read or watch, rather than constantly pushing deeper meanings.

As such, I hope that you have enjoyed this book. I have shared many thoughts, some you may agree with, and some you may have not. That's okay. The point of publishing a book like this is not to end the conversation, but to stimulate further discussion.

I hope it has helped you on the way to analysing horror yourself. Horror Studies is a new and emerging field of study, but is one that is not given the integrity it deserves. Whilst horror theorists are coming to the forefront, there are not enough of them to give the subject the precedence it needs. For example, you will never find a university degree course in Horror Studies—but I live in hope that, one day, you might.

And, hopefully, it will be myself leading it.

I will leave a list of books you might wish to read if you would like to continue learning about horror theory, or wish to explore some themes mentioned in this book.

Good luck with your studies—and remember to enjoy it. After all, there's nothing quite like a good bit of horror, is there?

FURTHER READING

To Do with Horror

'Robin Wood on the Horror Film Collected Essays and Reviews' edited by Keith Grant—a book of essays by the leading horror theorist.

'In the Dust of This Planet' by Eugene Thacker—discussions to do with the horror and philosophy, with a very interesting chapter on demons.

'Why Horror Seduces' by Mathias Clasen, on an evolutionary psychology perspective of why we find horror enjoyable.

To Do with Psychology and Philosophy

'A Little History of Philosophy' by Nigel Warburton—a summary of the most prominent philosophy theories throughout history.

'The Murderer Next Door' by David M. Buss—a study on how we are all capable of murder.

'Human Kind' by Rutger Bregman—a book that will restore your faith in humanity.

AND ME

'How to Write an Awesome Novel'—a book I wrote about how to craft your novel from first draft to final word.

And of course, you can find links to all my books on my website rickwoodwriter.com

Join Rick's Reader's Group and some free books!

Join now at www.rickwoodwriter.com/sign-up

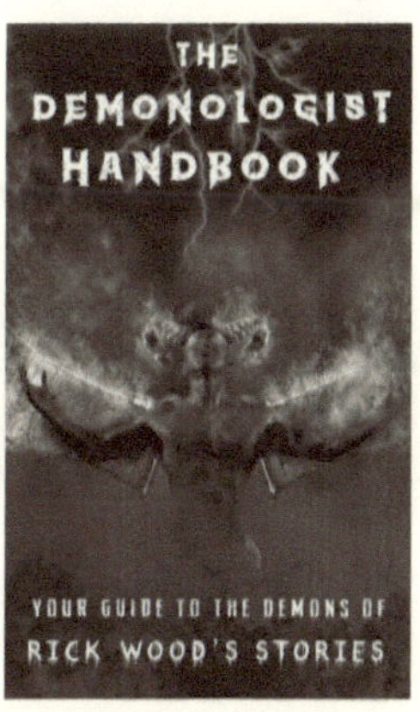

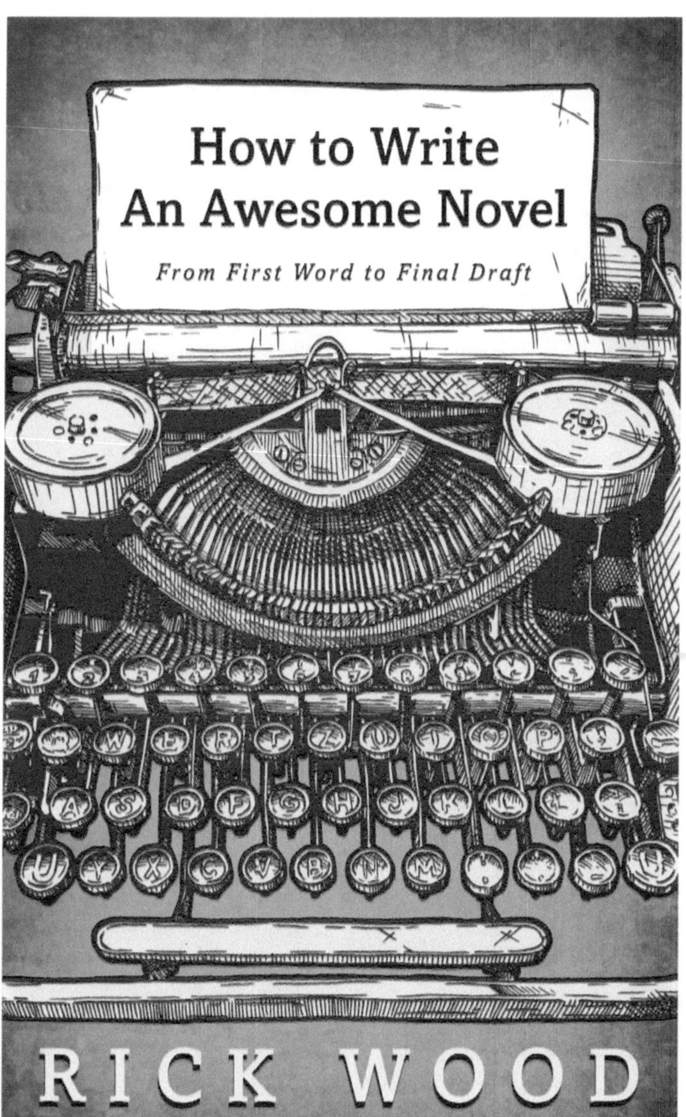

How to Write
An Awesome Novel
From First Word to Final Draft
RICK WOOD

BOOK ONE IN THE SENSITIVES SERIES
THE SENSITIVES
RICK WOOD

BLOOD SPLATTER BOOKS
18+
SEX
BLOOD
RICK WOOD

RICK WOOD
WHEN THE WORLD HAS ENDED
CIA ROSE BOOK ONE